When
the
Smoke
Cleared

Attica
Prison
Poems
and
Journal

Celes
Tisdale,
editor

with an introduction
by mark nowak

When the Smoke Cleared

Duke University Press Durham and London 2022

Betcha Ain't: Poems from Attica previously published
by Broadside Press, 1974.
Republished with a new preface and introduction and additional
poems and journal entries by Duke University Press, 2022.
© 2022 Duke University Press
Printed in the United States of America on acid-free paper ∞
Designed by Aimee C. Harrison
Typeset in Untitled Serif and Degular by Copperline Book Services

Library of Congress Cataloging-in-Publication Data
Names: Tisdale, Celes, [date] editor, compiler. | Nowak, Mark,
[date] writer of introduction.
Title: When the smoke cleared : Attica prison poems and journal /
edited by Celes Tisdale ; with an introduction by Mark Nowak.
Description: Durham : Duke University Press, 2022.
Identifiers: LCCN 2022007452 (print) | LCCN 2022007453 (ebook)
ISBN 9781478016304 (hardcover)
ISBN 9781478018940 (paperback)
ISBN 9781478023579 (ebook)
Subjects: LCSH: Prisoners' writings, American. | American
poetry—New York (State)—Attica. | Prisons—New York
(State)—Attica—Poetry. | Imprisonment—Poetry. |
BISAC: POETRY / American / African American & Black |
SOCIAL SCIENCE / Ethnic Studies / American / African
American & Black Studies
Classification: LCC PS591.P7 W44 2022 (print) |
LCC PS591.P7 (ebook) | DDC 811/.60809206927—dc23
/eng/20220422
LC record available at https://lccn.loc.gov/2022007452
LC ebook record available at https://lccn.loc.gov/2022007453

Cover art: From the Elizabeth Fink Papers.

I dedicate this to my wife, Tujuana K. Tucker-Tisdale, without whose foresight and encouragement I could not have completed this offering. And to the men in the Attica Correctional Facility Writers Workshop, whose humanity surpassed much of what I have ever experienced, I dedicate this completion of my journey into their insight and creativity.

Contents

Betcha Ain't: Poems from Attica

Celes Tisdale's Attica Poem and Journal

When the Smoke Cleared: More Poems from Attica

Preface

It was a cool fall afternoon, Thursday, September 9, 1971. I was thirty years old, walking across the campus of State University College at Buffalo, having finished teaching a class in the English Department. The Vietnam War was still America's burden; the feminist movement was necessary; the Black Arts Movement spoke for African Americans' identity in the arts, politics, and reflections of Africa; and Black Power advocates were speaking loudly. The Woodstock Arts Festival of 1969 was a recent memory, as was the tumultuous 1968 Democratic National Convention. Affirmation or denial of philosophical positions among American citizens often spawned protests, as did Vietnam, women's liberation, and Black Power identity. President John F. Kennedy, Robert Kennedy, Dr. Martin Luther King Jr., and Malcolm X had been assassinated, and fire hoses and dogs had been loosed on Black protesters for civil rights.

So on the cool fall afternoon of September 9, 1971, a student stopped me as I crossed the Buffalo State campus and asked, "Did you hear about the uprising at Attica State Prison?" And, as is said, the rest is history. One year later, I was at Attica Correctional Facility as the teacher of, I believe, the first poetry workshop in an American prison led by a non-inmate and African American.

Discoveries in poetry were made by the men as I discovered how deep their humanity was and how their dignity and respect shone. For three years, 1972 to 1975, almost every Wednesday, I made the thirty-five-mile trip to Attica to do what I loved (and still love) deeply: teach literature, especially poetry.

In 1974, the first major Black-owned publishing house in America, Broadside Press in Detroit, Michigan, published *Betcha Ain't*, which contained the poetry of the workshop members and my journal. The men insisted that we try to get their poetry published, and I agreed, especially after the encouragement of Broadside Press's owner, Dudley Randall, and poet Gwendolyn Brooks in 1974.

In 1982, Gwendolyn Brooks sent me a letter asking my forgiveness for keeping my manuscript "Every Wednesday" so long for her evaluation and comments. The manuscript was intended as a follow-up publication to *Betcha Ain't* and was so titled because of my weekly visits to Attica on Wednesday evenings. She suggested that I publish it on my own if no publishing house accepted it. Further, she recalled in her letter our trip together from Buffalo, New York, to the Attica Correctional Facility Writers Workshop's Wednesday-evening session in 1974. In her profoundly poetic way, she did not mention the poetry workshop but commented on the "clean store" in which we had ice-cream cones during the journey.

Gwendolyn Brooks was the first African American Pulitzer Prize winner, receiving the award for poetry in 1950 for *Annie Allen* (1949), which tells, in poetry, about the life of an African American girl growing to adulthood and motherhood in Chicago. I was "adopted" by Gwendolyn Brooks, and we shared a friendship of more than twenty-five years until her death in 2000.

And here we are, some fifty years later, with the follow-up publication to *Betcha Ain't* now called *When the Smoke Cleared: Attica Prison Poems and Journal*. I encouraged the men to know their worth and take pride in their work, but more importantly, I wanted the world to know them as poets of pride and confidence in this offering.

Thank you for reading the hearts of these men, and remember just that: they are men of courage who brought the world into their sphere.

Remember this.

—Celes Tisdale

Introduction

Celes Tisdale's Poetry Workshop at Attica

Mark Nowak

Black smoke billows into the sky from inside the high prison walls. More than 1,300 rioting prisoners have set fire to the carpenter's shop and other buildings. Police officers armed with hand grenades, tear gas, rifles, machine guns, and shotguns keep the prisoners at bay, while terrified townspeople buy up every firearm and bullet at the local hardware store, then join the prison guards along the wall to keep the rebellious prisoners contained. Unlike the officers and the townspeople, the prisoners possess no firearms. Prisoners who survive the riot will later recount stories of buckshot wounds they sustained in the uprising. Several hours after it begins, prison guards, police, and armed local townspeople succeed in quelling the riot. Dead bodies are transported to the local morgue.

To those familiar with the Attica prison uprising that occurred between September 9 and September 13, 1971, many of these details might sound familiar. The story above, however, is about the Dannemora prison uprising in the Adirondack region of northern New York on July 22, 1929.[1]

Six days after the uprising at Dannemora, the incarcerated men at Auburn Prison, near the central New York city of Syracuse, lead another rebellion in which three prisoners and two prison guards are killed. The next day, Franklin Delano Roosevelt, the governor of New York State, visits Dannemora; the following day, he visits Great Meadow Prison in Comstock, New York. After concluding his prison visits, FDR declares that the state must modernize its prisons in "a simple act of humanity." He continues, "The time has come when New York can no longer tolerate prisons like Dannemora and Auburn."[2]

Roosevelt was not, of course, preaching prison abolition. Yet, during his visits, he apparently saw some of what journalist Hastings H. Hart would describe, in the days after Roosevelt's visits, as the root causes of these New York State prison uprisings of 1929: overcrowding, scant wages for prison work, nearly inedible food, poorly trained prison staff, overly stern sentencing, indeterminate penal service, and more.[3] Conditions like these, it seems, have always been endemic to the carceral state.

Attica State Prison, or Attica Correctional Facility, as it was renamed in 1970, was born from the 1929 riots at Dannemora and Auburn. According to M. M. Wilmer, writing in the *New York Times* in January 1930, the riots made the construction of the new $12 million prison in the western New York village of Attica, thirty miles east of Buffalo, both necessary and urgent:

> If the succession of prison mutinies in this State have no other effect, they have directed an exceptional amount of attention to the new State prison under construction at Attica. . . . Whatever may be the outcome of the agitation, the immediate and practical answer to the convict revolts has been the new Attica prison. . . . The very slow progress that had been made toward building the institution before the riots contrasts with the energy that has been shown since those events.[4]

Some reporters in the months that followed would focus their stories on the daunting architecture of the fortresslike, soon-to-open prison in western New York. Attica, they wrote, had thirty-foot exterior walls and state-of-the-art keyless pneumatic locks. Other journalists, no doubt as balm for a nervous society or propaganda for Roosevelt's desire for prison reforms, called the new prison planned for Attica a "convict's paradise." Attica prisoners would soon be treated to spring beds, radios, and a cafeteria: "The village of Attica takes as much pride in [its new prison] as Niagara Falls does in its cataract, and Gettysburg its battlefield."[5] This comparison to the location of the military battle that resulted in the largest number of casualties in the Civil War would not age well.

Attica would see escapes, protests, and uprisings of its own soon after it received its first prisoner on July 1, 1931. Two and a half weeks later, Jesse S. Conklin, serving a ten-year term for forgery, became the first person to escape from Attica. Police arrested Conklin a week later after he stole a car in Wilawana, Pennsylvania.[6] Then, on the evening of De-

MARK NOWAK

cember 6, 1932, the first reported uprising of Attica prisoners occurred. Guards used tear gas to extinguish the rebellion, though Warden William Hurt would later deny use of the gas. Hurt blamed the first uprising at Attica on new arrivals from Sing Sing and "a strong distaste among certain other convicts for pick and shovel work."[7] At the end of that same month, another uprising occurred. The warden again denied it. According to Hurt, "One shot of the [tear] gas ended the demonstration."[8] Smaller work stoppages, demonstrations, and mass legal actions occurred at Attica in the following decades, from a "sour milk sit-down strike" by more than seven hundred prisoners in 1957 to the filing of more than one hundred court actions in 1961 by Black Muslims who were demanding religious freedom at the prison. In 1962, five thousand prisoners from at least four New York State prisons found a way to organize a coordinated, multiprison sit-in over a parole bill.[9]

The uprising at Attica in September 1971, the deadliest prison uprising in U.S. history, did not occur in a vacuum. In 1970 and the first months of 1971, prisoners across the country organized and launched a wave of prison escapes, occupations, strikes, and riots.[10] The movement reached one of its nadirs on August 21, 1971, when two guards shot and killed George Jackson at San Quentin State Prison. The murder of Jackson, author of *Soledad Brother* and a field marshal for the Black Panther Party, had an immediate impact on prisoners across the United States. The following day at Attica, for example, prisoners wore black mourning bands and refused to speak or eat as they staged a "spiritual sit-in" for Jackson.[11]

On the morning of September 9, 1971, as Heather Ann Thompson writes in *Blood in the Water: The Attica Prison Uprising of 1971 and Its Legacy*, nearly 1,300 prisoners took control of the prison's D Yard and transformed the yard into "an organized tent city with democratically elected representatives, a security force, a dining area, and a fairly well-equipped medical station."[12] The prisoners drafted a list of demands, a list influenced by the Attica Liberation Faction's "Manifesto of Demands and Anti-Depression Platform," which was inspired by a similar list written by prisoners at Folsom State Prison in California.[13] During the D Yard occupation, a prisoner spokesperson named L. D. Barkley, who was jailed at Attica for cashing a forged check and driving without a license, presented these demands to prison commissioner Russel G. Oswald and a group of journalists from the *New York Times*, the *Buffalo News*, NBC, ABC, and elsewhere who had joined Oswald to meet the negotiating team. The demands addressed economic, educational, religious, and political grievances that were not unlike those of the rebellions at Dannemora and Auburn prisons in 1929. The Attica prisoners wanted the New York State minimum wage to be paid for their mandatory prison labor; they wanted true religious freedom and cessation of the censorship of their reading materials (newspapers, magazines, etc.); they wanted an overhaul of the prison educational system and, as the demands expanded in the following days, a vastly transformed prison library.

L. D. Barkley and many of his fellow Attica prisoners in the D Yard would never see these demands for prison justice realized. On the morning of September 13, at approximately 10:00 a.m., Oswald, with the backing of Governor Nelson Rockefeller, ordered the retaking of the prison. Military helicopters first blanketed D Yard with CS gas (which induces almost immediate nausea and vomiting and is banned by the Geneva Conventions). Then, more than 450 New York State troopers, Attica guards, and sheriffs from nearby counties stormed the prison; they fired more than 4,500 rounds that included shotgun pellets and dumdum bullets (also outlawed by the Geneva Conventions).[14] They killed thirty-two prisoners and ten prison guards being held as hostages. An autopsy would find that L. D. Barkley was shot in the back—not during this initial assault, but later at close range. The bullet, "a badly fragmented jacketed bullet of slightly greater than 25 caliber," had lodged in the fourth rib on Barkley's right side and punctured his right lung. According to prisoners, as well as New York State assemblyman Arthur Eve, who had been part of the negotiating team, Barkley had been alive more than an hour after troops had taken control of the prison.[15]

Why did wages for prison labor become a central demand during both the 1929 and 1971 uprisings? Why did L. D. Barkley and his fellow Attica prisoners include in their list of demands a new educational model for prison classes? In the small number of classes already taught at prisons across New York State at the time, almost exclusively by white male teachers, lessons only reinforced the disjunct in the lived experience of Black life under white state surveillance that the prisoners experienced in their lives both inside and outside of Attica. A few of the white male teachers in the New York State prison system, it should be noted, also spoke out about the blatant racism of the white male prison guards and the prison education system in general. John Calhoun taught art at Eastern New York Correctional Facility in the Catskills town of Napanoch, where prisoners staged a memorial protest for their brothers at Attica. Prior to earning his art degree from the State University of New York, Calhoun had worked as a prison guard.[16] He spoke directly about the racism of the guards at prisons in New York:

> You see correctional officers walking around with their metal American flags. . . . Well, every American is entitled to show the flag. But that's not why they're wearing it. It's like every American is entitled to a sheet, but when he slits it and puts it over his head, then I know what he's thinking.[17]

Barkley and his fellow prisoners at Attica made trade union demands, Black Power movement demands, and abolitionist demands; they demanded new libraries and new teaching practices, class offerings, and teachers; they demanded uncensored books and magazines. They did not put their lives on the line in September 1971 for minor tweaks to the prison system.

Eight months after the brutal end of the Attica uprising, Celes Tisdale, a Black poet, new father, and professor at Buffalo State College, stepped through the front gates of Attica Correctional Facility. In his leather briefcase, which cleared security, he carried several books with poems by his favorite poets. One of these poems, Langston Hughes's "Ballad of the Landlord," spoke about a Black apartment tenant who is given ninety days in jail for refusing to pay rent until his landlord fixes his dilapidated apartment. Black life, Hughes's poem suggests, had long been linked with state incarceration. Tisdale described his initial impressions of Attica in his journal on the first day of his poetry workshop on May 24, 1972. The first words he writes about his arrival at Attica capture the mood at the prison: "The air is hot, still, restless." When I asked him what he most remembered about that first day at Attica, he answered with just one sentence: "You could still smell the smoke."[18]

Celes Tisdale was born on July 31, 1941, in Salters, South Carolina, a small farming community about seventy miles north of Charleston.[19] He was delivered by a midwife named Auntie Nellie, his grandmother once told him, who smoked a corncob pipe. His father, Norman Tisdale, worked with Celes's grandfather Paul Tisdale as a sharecropper. Shortly after Celes was born, his father and mother moved the family to Buffalo, New York, where Tisdale's five younger siblings would later be born. Tisdale credits his mother, Rachel, for his early love of poetry: "My mother was more of an artistic type. She liked poetry and read poetry to me, especially the poetry of Paul Laurence Dunbar." Norman Tisdale's uncle worked at Semet-Solvay, a coke oven plant in the north Buffalo industrial suburb of Tonawanda, and he got Norman a job there as a coke handler.

In 1942, after living with Norman's uncle Christopher Barr for a brief period, the expanding Tisdale family moved into a new apartment in Willert Park Courts on Buffalo's East Side. Tisdale remembers those days fondly. "There was a park where we played basketball right there, in the projects. There was a wading pool." Ishmael Reed was his next-door neighbor.[20] A library was part of the housing complex, too, "in the basement where we paid our rent," as Tisdale recalls. "And that's where I spent a lot of my time. I was a voracious reader." All this time in the library earned him his childhood nickname: "The Professor." More than fifty years after he last lived there, the abandoned Willert Park Courts have been placed on the National Trust for Historic Preservation's list of "11 Most Endangered Places." The trust describes Willert Park as "one of the first garden/courtyard housing projects in the nation"; it also cites its "distinctive bas-relief sculptures depicting scenes of African American life and achievement . . . developed in cooperation with the first residents of the complex."[21]

Tisdale attended Public School 31 and Seneca Vocational High School. His dream was to become an electrician because he had a passion for the emerging medium of television. As he neared his high school graduation in 1959, Tisdale hoped to train for his future career in the air force. But his guidance counselor at Seneca noticed his outstanding grades (especially in English and history) and helped him get into Buffalo State College on Buffalo's West Side. He remembers being one of only two Black English majors on the campus. During his college years, Tisdale worked at Willert Park Drugs and the Panama Lunch (known locally as Smitty's restaurant after its owner, Alfred Smith). He worked in the kitchen every Sunday from 8:00 a.m. to 8:00 p.m. for $20, and through these two jobs, he paid for his college education. Tisdale earned a BA in English in 1963, then returned to PS 31 as an English teacher. He would also earn an MA in English from Buffalo State in 1969 and continue his PhD studies at the University of Buffalo.

During the 1960s, Tisdale began participating in the burgeoning arts scene in Buffalo's Black community. He became a member of the Buffalo Black Drama Workshop, founded by director Ed Smith, who had moved to Buffalo from Philadelphia. Tisdale also founded the Nia Writers Workshop (*Nia* from the Swahili word for intention or purpose). During this time, Tisdale performed extensively in regional Black theater productions, and he wrote and performed his own poetry inspired by Black Arts Movement poets like Amiri Baraka and Sonia Sanchez, Beat poets like Lawrence Ferlinghetti, and of course his mother's favorite poet, Paul Laurence Dunbar.

A few months after the Attica uprising, Randy Lerner, an arts administrator at Hospital Audiences Inc., a nonprofit based in New York City, approached the Black Drama Workshop about an idea for a new program. Hospital Audiences wanted to offer a creative writing workshop at Attica, and Lerner recruited Tisdale from the Black Drama Workshop to lead the program. Tisdale remembers sitting on his porch on the afternoon of his first trip to Attica and trying to imagine what it would be like to enter the prison he had seen almost daily the previous fall on the cover of the *Buffalo Evening News*. After Lerner picked him up, they made the thirty-five-mile drive to Attica together. The history of this day and all of Tisdale's Attica poetry workshop classes is documented in his journal.

The poems and journal entries in *When the Smoke Cleared* are published here as Tisdale had intended in the 1970s: the original poems from *Betcha Ain't: Poems from Attica*, edited by Tisdale and originally published in 1974 by Dudley Randall's Detroit-based Broadside Press, one of the most important publishing houses for Black literature in the twentieth century; Tisdale's journal from *Betcha Ain't* with an additional thirty-nine journal entries not included in the original volume; and twenty previously unpublished Attica poems from Tisdale's personal archive, originally collected in a second manuscript titled "Every Wednesday" (named after the day of his weekly workshop at Attica).[22] These poems and expanded journal entries are published here together for the first time, fifty years after they were first written.

Betcha Ain't was the first Black Arts Movement prison anthology dedicated solely to poetry to be published in the United States. Tisdale's journal tells the story from that first night of the Attica workshop on May 24, 1972, when, he writes, "I recognize[d] some of [my students] from the old days in Willert Park Projects and Smitty's restaurant," to his return to Attica on June 12, 1974, with copies of *Betcha Ain't* in hand to give to the workshop participants who were still at Attica (some participants had been transferred to other prisons or released). In one of the earliest journal entries, from June 7, 1972—one that was not included in *Betcha Ain't* but is published here for the first time—Tisdale describes the workshop participants' excitement as they discuss the news that prison abolitionist Angela Davis had been found not guilty in the Marin County Civic Center kidnapping trial.[23] Tisdale says he chose not to get "involved in a political discussion" with his students—in part because guards were often present in the sessions and, as leader of this brand-new program, Tisdale was concerned about his Attica workshop being censored or canceled. Instead, he funneled the discussion of Davis's release through poetry, asking his students to read and discuss Nikki Giovanni's "Poem of Angela Yvonne Davis." While overt political discussions might raise suspicions in prison guards and administrators, who would be suspicious of a small group of students sitting around a table and talking about a poem?

In another previously unpublished entry, Tisdale writes on July 20, 1972, about the cancellation of his poetry workshop after Superintendent Ernest L. Montanye declared a state of emergency at the prison. According to Tisdale, approximately nine hundred prisoners refused to leave their cells due to the termination of a nurse, and their protest successfully led to the nurse being reinstated. In the same entry, Tisdale mentions his workshop students' desire to publish a book. He also writes that Randy Lerner, from the sponsoring organization, Hospital Audiences Inc., became "very apprehensive" about continuing the poetry workshop after this initial eight-week session because "many prisoners' protests continue." Although it is not included in his journal, Tisdale did corroborate a story in the *New York Times* that mentions his workshop in relation to another post-1971 protest at Attica.[24] On November 7, 1972, students in Tisdale's workshop read poems as part of a Black Solidarity Day program at Attica, which, the *New York Times* stated, included "a series of talks by prisoners, staff members of the prison and a volunteer director of a

MARK NOWAK

black poetry workshop at the prison." The article quotes Superintendent Montanye: "'Some of the talks were fairly militant,' Mr. Montanye said, 'and a few of the prisoners may have misinterpreted them.'"[25] The following afternoon, fifty prisoners "joined hands and shouted slogans in the exercise yard." Prison officials immediately removed the guards from the yard. Approximately thirty guards in riot gear—armed with tear gas, shotguns, and batons—then headed to the roof atop the prison corridor from which shooting the previous year had commenced. According to the newspaper story, Montanye spoke to the protesters in the exercise yard through a bullhorn to eventually defuse the situation—this time without the use of tear gas and gunfire.[26] These two stories from the summer and fall of 1972 give just a small glimpse into the tense conditions at Attica during the time of Tisdale's workshop.

Tisdale's journal entries give readers a unique opportunity to experience what it was like to enter Attica as a poet-educator and to return, week after week, to discuss poetry with the participants in his workshop. In one particularly insightful entry from March 14, 1973, also published here for the first time, Tisdale discusses the workshop's precarity. Just ten months after it started, funding for the Attica program through the Black Drama Workshop had been cut, and attendance had dropped to only three writers, "two of whom were new"—a problem Tisdale assigned to "administrative laxity." Yet even during what he believed on that particular Wednesday night to be "maybe [the] last eight-week session," Tisdale finds hope. He introduces his participants to the "Tis-O-Gram" (see appendix), an exercise Tisdale invented to help his students convert abstract ideas and emotions into concrete examples—the classic "show, don't tell" mantra of creative writing teachers everywhere.

The Tis-O-Gram uses a grid system. In the leftmost column, Tisdale lists more than twenty abstract ideas: love, hate, fear, disappointment, pain, trust, poverty, violence, and so on. Then, across the grid in separate columns Tisdale asks his students to provide an example of what each of these abstract ideas "looks like," "smells like," "tastes like," "sounds like," and "feels like (to touch)" and what "color" it is. A note at the bottom of the Tis-O-Gram instructs: "Responses should be one word; no response should be used more than once." The Tis-O-Gram encourages beginning writers like his students at Attica to use a wide range of concrete imagery, colors, shapes, smells, and sounds in their poems. Does *fear* sound like breaking glass or someone slamming a door? Does *joy* smell like pancakes or a paycheck? Is *anxiety* deep purple or lemon yellow? With the Tis-O-Gram, Tisdale sought a method for helping those who had lived through the Attica uprising to turn their experiences into vivid, well-crafted, and compelling poems.

In addition to the Tis-O-Gram, Tisdale brought the rich history of Black poetry to his workshop at Attica. During the second eight-week session, for example, students read and analyzed poems in *The Black Poets*, an anthology edited by Dudley Randall and published the previous year (the year of the Attica uprising). Randall's comprehensive anthology begins with "Folk Poetry" (which Randall divides into "Folk Seculars" and "Spirituals"), then transitions into "Literary Poetry" with early Black writers such as Phillis Wheatley, James Weldon Johnson, and Celes Tisdale's mother's favorite poet, Paul Laurence Dunbar. Further sections cover the Harlem Renaissance, the Post-Renaissance, and the Black Arts Movement poets of the 1960s.[27] Tisdale supplemented this last section by playing albums by poets of the Black Arts Movement including Nikki Giovanni (*Truth Is on Its Way*), Amiri Baraka (whose album *It's Nation Time* was released during the first year of Tisdale's workshop), and The Last Poets (*The Last Poets*).[28]

Through these exercises and examples, both textual and musical, Tisdale joined an emerging movement of Black writers in the early 1970s who were seeking to establish a Black literary history and Black Arts Movement pedagogy specific to poetry writing. For example, *A Capsule Course in Black Poetry Writing*, originally scheduled to be published by Broadside Press in late 1971, collects essays by Gwendolyn Brooks, Keorapetse Kgositsile, Haki R. Madhubuti, and Dudley Randall.[29] As Randall writes in his brief introduction to *A Capsule Course*, "This handbook grew out of a suggestion by Gwendolyn Brooks that she compose a small textbook on writing poetry." The idea eventually expanded to include essays by other poets, an idea about which Randall claims he was "doubtful" (due to potentially contradictory writing advice). Randall summarizes the audience for this book as "beginning Black poets": "This is not a book for experienced writers. Only the rudiments of poetry are discussed."[30]

While Randall's summary holds true for Madhubuti's contribution as well as his own, the essays by Brooks and Kgositsile reach beyond introductory discussions of alliteration, rhythm, publishing, et cetera for beginners. In her contribution to *A Capsule Course*, Brooks urges new writers to subscribe to a new ideal: "The new black ideal italicizes black identity, black solidarity, black self-possession and self-address."[31] As she continues in a section that parallels many of the themes of poems collected in *When the Smoke Cleared*: "1966. 1967. 1968. Years of explosion. In those years a young black with pen in hand responded not to pretty sunsets and the lapping of lake water but to the speech of physical riot and spiritual rebellion." Later in the same passage, Brooks adds, "Sometimes the literature seemed to issue from pens dipped in, *stabbed* in, writhing blood."[32] In the final section of her essay, headed "A Few Hints toward the Making of Poetry," Brooks urges new poets to bring their personal histories into the poem. In one illuminating passage, she writes:

> If you allude to a star, say precisely what that star means to *you*. If you feature a garden, speak of that garden *most personally*. If you have murdered in a garden, the grass and flowers (and weeds) will mean something different to you than to someone who has only planted or picked.[33]

Brooks, who won the Pulitzer Prize for Poetry and taught poetry workshops with the Blackstone Rangers, invokes craft within a radical political context, radical politics with an aesthetic context, and the conjunction of craft and politics within the context of an emerging radical Black tradition in poetry pedagogy.[34]

Like Brooks, Kgositsile describes the very act of the study of creative writing as a deeply political practice. He asks, early in his essay in this primer for new Black poets, "How can you have a revolutionary literature without a revolution to form and inform, to shape and strengthen a writer's sensibility?"[35] This sentiment, of course, is far from the aesthetic of almost every poetry handbook of the times (or of today). He calls on the new Black writer to be a documentarian, a historian, a reporter: "If there is any validity to the making of a black poetry, as in the making in any other attempts in any other areas of our lives, the poetry has to explore and report exactly where we are." He calls out a need for "exposé-poems," poems that "report on and explore the tragedy of our times."[36] In this way, his insights echo C. L. R. James and Grace Lee Boggs's invocation to writers to "recognize and record."[37] In Brooks's and Kgositsile's essays in *A Capsule Course*, we find the central notion that radical politics conjoined to the documentation of everyday life must remain at the center of any new Black poet's practice.

In her introduction to *The New Abolitionists: (Neo)Slave Narratives and Contemporary Prison Writings*, Joy James expands on this idea by asserting that imprisoned Black writers, like the poets collected in *When the Smoke Cleared*, "function as progressive abolitionists and register as 'people's historians.' They become the storytellers of the political histories of the captives *and* their captors. These narratives are generally the 'unauthorized' versions of political life, often focusing on dissent and policing and repression."[38] The poets collected here, in James's terms, serve as the "people's historians" of the Attica prison uprising, men who experienced firsthand the events of September 9–13, 1971, and turned to poetry to write about that moment. These poets report on Black life in a prison monitored exclusively by white guards and a white administration. They also "recognize and record," more generally, Black life in America in the late 1960s and early 1970s.

The poets who attended Tisdale's workshop tell their version of the history of the Attica uprising throughout *When the Smoke Cleared*. Isaiah Hawkins's "13th of Genocide" documents September 13, 1971, by using six four-line stanzas to chronicle the day when "the white folks were coming / to lay some black brothers away." He describes how white state troopers and white sheriffs "from eight surrounding counties" amassed outside the walls of Attica on that day. Their message, Hawkins says, was clear:

> The word was kill niggers,
>   kill all you can
> For they don't have the right
>   to live like men.

Hawkins's people's history in poetic form is supported by outside sources. A year after the uprising, for example, one journalist reported that when the hundreds of state police officers ("not one who was black") stormed Attica and surged into D Yard the previous year, they were chanting, "White power, white power."[39]

Hawkins uses an array of poetic tools and devices that he learned about in Tisdale's workshop to describe and analyze this racism and police brutality through poetry: slant rhyme in the second and fourth lines of the stanza quoted above (can/men); the metaphor of a big green bird that represents the two state police helicopters, one of which flew over the prison and announced an order to surrender just moments before a second helicopter began to spray CS gas across D Yard as the prison take-over began. Hawkins's "big green bird" — a *Time* magazine article on the uprising called them "Viet Nam–style helicopters"[40] — speaks with a human voice:

> "Put your hands on your heads
> > and you won't get hurt,
> lie on your bellies,
> > put your face in the dirt."

Finally, Hawkins echoes Claude McKay's most famous poem, "If We Must Die," in the final stanza of his poem. Hawkins's narrator hears "a black brother's cry" in the distance as the massacre unfolds: "I'm a man, white folks, and like a man I'll die." Two weeks after the uprising, *Time* magazine mistakenly assigned the authorship of McKay's poem, which was found in the rubble after D Yard was cleared, to one of the prisoners. In a follow-up letter to the editor, Gwendolyn Brooks corrected the magazine's error.[41]

Rather than rhyming stanzas, a poem by Mshaka (Willie Monroe), "Formula for Attica Repeats," uses a jagged, stepped free verse line to narrate the day of the massacre.[42] Mshaka's analysis of the events of September 13, 1971, focuses on the violent moments after the uprising and the potential for political change in the future. For Mshaka, "when / the smoke cleared" signals the moment when the true brutality of the carceral system and the racism of the prison guards is unleashed upon the prisoners. In the minutes and hours after state forces took D Yard, prison guards stripped the surviving prisoners (also removing their eyeglasses and dentures) and forced them to run through a fifty-yard "gauntlet" where officers would beat the prisoners with "ax handles, 2 x 4s, baseball bats and rifle butts."[43] Mshaka accuses the guards of being refusers "of S.O.S. Collect Calls" and, in the end, the prisoners' "Executioner[s]." Despite this atrocity, despite the prison spokespeople and police who came as "tearless / tremblers" to deliver "state-prepared speeches" and other misinformation about the massacre, Mshaka sees in "the 43 dead men" the potential to again rise up for their dignity, for their demands, and even for the possibility of the eventual abolition of the oppressive system itself.

Of course, not every poem in *When the Smoke Cleared* is a documentary history of the uprising. Many other poems collected here reach beyond life in prison. L. Alexander Brooks's fantastical ballad, "The Odyssey of Louie Fats," is a story about love and desire set in the Brooklyn Navy Yard. Brooks and Harold E. Packwood write haiku, a three-line Japanese poetic form with a strict syllable count (5–7–5), while Packwood also employs a French poetic form, the cinquain (a five-line poem). Tisdale taught these forms to the poets in his workshop. Joseph Hardy ("Synopsis of a Hummingbird") and Christopher Sutherland ("The End of Summer") write about a more pastoral life, too.

Black music, particularly jazz, is also a frequent theme. The poets in Tisdale's workshop invoke jazz musicians such as Sun Ra, John Coltrane, and Miles Davis in several poems. As Tisdale mentions in a journal entry of July 5, 1972, his students that day were thrilled to have seen tenor saxophone legend Archie Shepp perform at Attica the previous night (Shepp's classic album *Attica Blues* was released that same year). Shepp was, as Amiri Baraka called him a few years earlier, "a tenor man of the new jazz, who came out of an American background of Black slums and white palaces. He is a Marxist playwrighting tenor-saxophone player now. . . . You hear in Archie's music moans that are pleas for understanding."[44] Christopher Sutherland heard Shepp's "pleas for understanding" when Shepp performed at Attica on the Fourth of July, aka "Independence Day," and Sutherland turned the inspiration of Shepp's performance into a poem that first appears in this volume, "Applause to Archie Shepp & Co."[45] For Sutherland, Shepp's moans and pleas are inscribed as a "rhythmic hope message." Similarly, in his poem "'Olé,'" Harold E. Packwood, who was also a saxophone player, conjures the "blasting horns" of John Coltrane, Eric Dolphy, and Miles Davis as well as the "cosmic/chord" struck by Sun Ra.

Other poems speak more generally about the Black revolutionary politics of the late 1960s and early 1970s. John Lee Norris's "/PRISON POETS/," published here for the first time, exemplifies the influence of the Black Arts Movement in the Attica workshop. Norris places the all-caps title to his poem between two slashes; even Norris's title is visually between or behind bars.[46] Readers of Norris's poem might hear echoes of

Baraka's "Black Art," mentioned by many literary critics as one of the more important poems of the Black Arts Movement and a poem that Tisdale taught in his Attica workshop.[47] William J. Harris, in *The Poetry and Poetics of Amiri Baraka: The Jazz Aesthetic*, asserts that in "Black Art" Baraka wanted to write a new kind of poem that "had to be an active agent, not a vehicle of escape to 'another world.'"[48] Baraka spoke in a similar way in his autobiography: "I wanted to go 'beyond' poetry. I wanted to write some kind of action literature."[49]

Baraka famously begins "Black Art" by declaring: "Poems are bullshit unless they are / Teeth or trees or lemons piled / On a step." Norris similarly uses the image of teeth in his opening lines, stating that "black / poems / about / prisons / should have   teeth that bite." Violence against oppressors (cops, prison guards, the racist state, etc.) forms a clear theme in both poems. In "Black Art," Baraka calls for

> Assassin poems, Poems that shoot
> Guns. Poems that wrestle cops into alleys
> And take their weapons leaving them dead
> With tongues pulled out and sent to Ireland.

The teeth of Norris's opening lines also become active agents: "black / poets / in / prisons should bite ass." Norris's poem, of course, doesn't have the sweeping arc of Baraka's "Black Art" and its concluding call-out to "poems & poets & / All the loveliness here in the world." Norris, writing from inside Attica, ends his poem more abruptly, invoking active agents (i.e., the prison poets of the title) who will work to eradicate the systems of prison sublimation. Black poets in prison, as he writes in his concluding lines, need to "pile / zebra / stripes / bodiesbetweenthelines."

While important literary studies of the Black Arts Movement and several of its central writers (particularly Amiri Baraka) have been published to date, few studies have examined the role of the Black Arts Movement aesthetic in prison writing workshops during this period.[50] *Who Took the Weight? Black Voices from Norfolk Prison*, for example, displays the ways prison writing workshops taught by Black writers and teachers expanded notions of craft, politics, pedagogy, and poetic practice.[51] *Who Took the Weight?* collects poems, essays, stories, and plays from ten prisoners who enrolled in Elma Lewis's Technical Theater Training Program at Massachusetts Correctional Institution at Norfolk (dubbed the Norfolk Penal

Colony by those it incarcerated). The volume was edited by an anonymous group of workshop members calling itself the Norfolk Prison Brothers and was published in 1972, the year that Tisdale began his workshop at Attica.

The Norfolk workshop participants invited Lewis to the prison, as she writes in her foreword, because they felt a need "for an education about the black experience" that they had failed to receive both in the schools they attended and from the few educational programs at the prison.[52] They saw programs on Black history and Black arts as essential not only for their time in prison, Lewis writes, but for a time when they returned to their communities, too:

> They would like their children, their brothers, their sisters, their mothers and fathers to sidestep the trap before it's sprung. They teach the development of alternatives. They no longer see through a glass darkly. They would like to see their communities move toward ownership and control. They hope to pass along the revelation to blacks in all black communities.[53]

Like Black Arts Movement poets, the prisoners who occupied D Yard at Attica in September 1971, and people in Black communities across the United States, the writers in Lewis's Norfolk prison workshop sought, through their education, to be able to learn for themselves and teach others in their communities about self-determination and solidarity, about alternatives and ownership, about community control and creative writing, too.[54]

Similar to the poems created in Tisdale's workshop, the poems, plays, short stories, and essays collected in *Who Took the Weight?* address a wide range of political, cultural, and social concerns. The book opens with a dedication: "To Jonathan Jackson and the Soledad Brothers & to the brothers in Attica, who gave their lives in order for us to live! a little longer." The opening poem by Sayif, for example, interlaces Muslim spirituality and Black music. Juno Bakali Tshombe / Craig Dee Anderson's "Attempt—or The Reason Why the Revolution / Is Getting Off to a Bad Start," the next poem in the anthology, alludes to the cosmic jazz so prevalent in the early 1970s in its references to "black rhythm," "cosmic rays of black solidarity," and "a universal plane / of black corrective thinking."[55] Like Tisdale's anthology, *Who Took the Weight?* includes a wide range of poetic styles: love poems, jazz/bop-inspired free verse, rhyming stanzas, polemical tracts, and so on. However, there is significantly less attention to traditional poetic forms like the haiku, cinquain, and ballad that Tisdale taught.

Lewis's workshop at Massachusetts Correctional Institution at Norfolk not only created a space for Black prisoners to write creatively and produce dramatic works; her workshop gave Black prisoners a vehicle for creating an alternative educational space for Black political and creative transformation. In his essay "Psychological Warfare at Norfolk Prison Camp," Juno Bakali Tshombe / Craig Dee Anderson summarizes the vital lifeline provided by prison workshops like this one:

> There is no program other than Elma Lewis's here that is working towards attaining some degree of thinking and a positive direction that will relate to the confined black prisoner and offer him a productive analysis needed for self-awareness and racial awareness. . . .
>
> Clearly the administration is thinking in terms of "let them niggers put on some plays describing their condition to each other or write poetry that no one gives a damn about, but under no circumstances whatsoever let them produce anything with any political overtones." This is what the European settler's prison system is bent on beating back into the furthest regions of the black prisoner's psyche, for it is here that the black man encounters the extreme in white racist persecution. Here the guard dog is in an environment that refuses to check his racism unless there is one of those "mild investigations" going on.[56]

Prison writing workshops of the early 1970s, however, did create a space for what Robin D. G. Kelley calls the "black radical imagination."[57] They created spaces for writing with "political overtones"; they became a vehicle for Black prisoners to, as Joy James said, "become the storytellers of the political histories of the captives *and* their captors."[58] And the racism, violence, and brutality of these captors certainly wasn't an image that those who controlled the system wanted in public view. Yet the poetry workshops and the anthologies that came out of them became a way for the prisoners' writings about the carceral state's racist, dehumanizing, and brutal history to be published for all to read.

In the end, however, no writers other than the poets included here have collectively documented their personal experiences during the Attica uprising through poetry.[59] This is what makes the poems in *When the Smoke Cleared* so unique. Hersey Boyer's "Attica Reflections" documents prisoners like himself weeping in "the silence / Of midnights" in the aftermath of the retaking of the prison. "They have witnessed the slaughter," he writes, yet he has also seen the white prison guards sing "songs of merriment" as they "filled [their] cups with blood" in the running of the gauntlet and other forms of violence in which the guards engaged after they secured the prison.[60] Daniel Brown uses the image of tears, too, as he wishes that tears could be empowered with agency: "If tears could destroy, / Our plight would cease."

Sam Washington repeats a pair of questions in the first three lines of each of the five stanzas in his poem "Was It Necessary": "Was it really necessary? / Did they really have to carry / Rifles and shotguns?"—questions we continue to ask in our current uprisings against the police murders of George Floyd, Breonna Taylor, Daunte Wright, and other unarmed Black people across the United States. In the opening stanza, Washington's narrator sarcastically replies, "Let's ask the gov', / Who's so full of love!," and this refrain is repeated as the closing couplet of all but the last stanza. In other lines, the narrator asks why such heavy artillery was used "Against sticks and knives!" Was it really necessary, Washington asks, to shoot "with intent to kill! / . . . even when they lay still!" He conveys his utter disdain for Governor Rockefeller, who refused to come to Attica during the uprising to speak with the prisoners or the negotiating team: "While troopers were killing with hate and glee, / Rock was safe in Albany!"

Finally, John Lee Norris's poem "Just Another Page," written from the perspective of the one-year anniversary of the Attica uprising, uses anaphora (the repetition of words at the beginning of a poetic line) to build from a flat, direct opening pair of lines ("A year later / And it's just another page") into a crescendo that viscerally inscribes the entirety of the Attica prison system and the racist government that oversees it:

> And Attica is a maggot-minded black blood sucker
> And the only thing they do right is wrong
> And another page of history is written in black blood
> And old black mamas pay taxes to buy guns that killed their sons
> And the consequence of being free . . . is death

But Norris doesn't ask for "your sympathy and tears" because, as he writes in the next line of his poem, those tears "always come too late." Instead, Norris urges action, abolition, radical change.

Sam Washington, John Lee Norris, and all the poets included in *When the Smoke Cleared* have declared themselves in these pages to be something more than simply prisoners incarcerated at Attica; they are poets, people's historians, husbands, documentarists, fathers, artists, brothers, uncles, and more. This book is meant to showcase their poetic achievements, their desire for self-determination, and their historical role as "the storytellers of the political histories of the captives *and* their captors" before, during, and after the Attica uprising.[61] Harold E. Packwood, in a letter he wrote to Tisdale from the prison on October 13, 1972, describes the deep impact of the poetry workshop on its participants: "Since the Workshop began, I have seen brothers' characters change, as well as their poetry. We have become more conscious of one another, and we've come closer together. Upon poetry we have built a common bond which will be hard to break."[62] As you read through the poems, remember this new space of radical Black creativity and solidarity that Celes Tisdale's poetry workshop created inside Attica Correctional Facility just a few months after the smoke cleared.

NOTES

1. Details in the opening paragraphs are taken from "3 Convicts Killed, 20 Hurt, 1,300 Riot at Dannemora," *New York Times*, July 23, 1929, 1.

2. "Roosevelt Urges Modern Prisons," *New York Times*, July 31, 1929, 1.

3. Hastings H. Hart, "What Lies behind the Outbreaks in Prisons," *New York Times*, August 4, 1929, 4.

4. M. M. Wilner, "New Attica Prison to Cost $12 Million," *New York Times*, January 26, 1930, 51.

5. "Attica Prison to Be Convicts' Paradise," *New York Times*, August 2, 1931, E5.

6. "Held for Attica Escape: Man Seized in Pennsylvania Said to Be First to Flee New Prison," *New York Times*, July 30, 1931, 20.

7. "Attica Convicts Riot; Damage Is Reported," *New York Times*, December 8, 1932, 13.

8. "Attica Prison Row Quelled by Tear Gas," *New York Times*, December 30, 1932, 8.

9. For the 1957 strike, see "'Sit-Down' in Prison: Attica Convicts Charge

They Were Given Sour Milk," *New York Times*, June 20, 1957, 22. For more on the Muslim lawsuits, see "Muslim Negroes Suing the State," *New York Times*, March 16, 1961, 1. For the coordinated strike of 1962, see "5,000 Prisoners Strike in State: Convicts at 4 Prisons Stage Sit-In over Parole Bill," *New York Times*, March 13, 1962, 32. And for a comprehensive historical account of the Attica prison uprising, see Heather Ann Thompson's Pulitzer Prize–winning book *Blood in the Water: The Attica Prison Uprising of 1971 and Its Legacy* (New York: Pantheon, 2016).

10. A detailed list of prison escapes, occupations, strikes, and riots in 1970–71 can be found on the website of the *Abolitionist*: "Prison Struggle 1970–1," March 9, 2012, https://abolitionistpaper.wordpress.com/2012/03/09/prison-struggle-1970-1-5/.

11. Thompson, *Blood in the Water*, 35–36.

12. Thompson, *Blood in the Water*, 69.

13. The Attica Liberation Faction's list of demands is printed in Samuel Melville, *Letters from Attica* (New York: William Morrow and Company, 1972), 175–81.

14. Jeff Z. Klein, "The Attica Prison Uprising—43 Dead and a Four-Decade Cover-Up," NPR, September 10, 2018, https://news.wbfo.org/post/heritage-moments-attica-prison-uprising-43-dead-and-four-decade-cover.

15. Thompson, *Blood in the Water*, 238.

16. "Prisoners Exhibit Paintings at New York Art Show," *Federal Probation: A Journal of Correctional Philosophy and Practice* 34, no. 1 (March 1970): 83.

17. Fred Ferretti, "Tension in Catskill Prison," *New York Times*, September 22, 1971, 51.

18. Interview with the author, September 12, 2019. I wrote briefly about Celes Tisdale's *Betcha Ain't: Poems from Attica* in my essay "Panthers, Patriots, and Poets in Revolution," published in *Organize Your Own: The Politics and Poetics of Self-Determination Movements*, ed. Anthony Romero (Chicago: Soberscove Press, 2016), 26–46. I was unable to locate Celes at that time. Materials from this essay eventually made it into a section on Celes Tisdale's Attica workshop in my book *Social Poetics* (Minneapolis: Coffee House Press, 2020). I was eventually able to get a current phone number for Tisdale from poet and professor Gene Grabiner (who took a poetry workshop I was facilitating with the Western New York Council on Occupational Safety and Health at the Just Buffalo Literary Center). Grabiner and Tisdale had been colleagues at Erie Community College. After several phone conversations, Celes invited me to his home in Georgia to read the previously unpublished materials he had in his archives. This first meeting at his house in Augusta occurred on September 12, 2019, exactly forty-seven years after the uprising. We have

continued to speak regularly since then as we worked on the publication of this book.

19. Tisdale's biographical information in this introduction is taken from a series of interviews and phone conversations we had between August 2019 and the time this book went to press in 2022.

20. Reed is the author of more than thirty award-winning novels, poetry volumes, and essay collections. His family lived at Willert Park Courts from its opening in 1937 until Reed's seventh-grade year. See "Ishmael Reed," Just Buffalo Literary Center, accessed January 13, 2022, https://www.justbuffalo .org/community/lit-city/ishmael-reed/. See also Nicola Paladin and Giorgio Rimondi, eds., *Una bussola per l'infosfera con Ishmael Reed tra musica e letteratura* (Milan: Agenzia X, 2017), which includes "Da Willert Park Courts a Palazzo Leoni Montanari," an address by Ishmael Reed (27–39).

21. "Press Release: Willert Park Courts," Preservation Buffalo Niagara, May 30, 2019, https://preservationbuffaloniagara.org/blog-post/press -release-willert-park-courts/.

22. For more on the history of Broadside Press, see Melba Joyce Boyd, *Wrestling with the Muse: Dudley Randall and the Broadside Press* (New York: Columbia University Press, 2003).

23. Philip Hager, "Angela Davis Not Guilty, Jury Finds," *Los Angeles Times*, June 5, 1972, 1.

24. Conversation with the author, May 29, 2020.

25. "50 Inmates of Attica Cause a Brief Disturbance," *New York Times*, November 10, 1972, 43.

26. "50 Inmates of Attica Cause a Brief Disturbance," 43.

27. Dudley Randall, ed., *The Black Poets* (New York: Bantam Press, 1971).

28. A file in Tisdale's archive lists him playing the Nikki Giovanni album in his class on August 23, 1972; Amiri Baraka on September 27, 1972; and The Last Poets on October 4, 1972.

29. As Randall writes in the introduction, "Some of the writers failed to meet the original deadline of December 1, 1971. The publication was delayed until 1975. Dudley Randall, introduction to *A Capsule Course in Black Poetry Writing* by Gwendolyn Brooks, Keorapetse Kgositsile, Haki R. Madhubuti, and Dudley Randall (Detroit: Broadside Press, 1975), 1.

30. Randall, introduction, 1.

31. Gwendolyn Brooks, untitled essay in Brooks et al., *A Capsule Course*, 3.

32. Brooks, in *A Capsule Course*, 4.

33. Brooks, in *A Capsule Course*, 10.

34. For more on the Blackstone Rangers, see Natalie Y. Moore and Lance Williams, *The Almighty Black P Stone Nation: The Rise, Fall, and Resurgence of an American Gang* (Chicago: Chicago Review Press, 2011).

35. Keorapetse Kgositsile, untitled essay in Brooks et al., *A Capsule Course*, 12.

36. Kgositsile, in *A Capsule Course*, 13.

37. C. L. R. James and Grace C. Lee (Boggs) with the collaboration of Cornelius Castoriadis, *Facing Reality* (1958; Detroit: Bewick Editions, 1974), 131.

38. Joy James, "Introduction: Democracy and Captivity," in *The New Abolitionists: (Neo)Slave Narratives and Contemporary Prison Writings*, ed. Joy James (Albany: State University of New York Press, 2005), xxxii.

39. Jack Newfield, "An Anniversary for Attica," *New York Times*, September 13, 1972, 47.

40. "War at Attica: Was There No Other Way?," *Time*, September 27, 1971, 18.

41. David Caplan, *Questions of Possibility: Contemporary Poetry and Poetic Form* (Oxford: Oxford University Press, 2005), 11–12:

> [Claude McKay's poem] even made *Time* magazine after a reporter discovered it in the Attica State prison following the September 1971 uprising, the largest penal rebellion in American history. Reading the sonnet as a call to action, the prisoners circulated it to each other, along with banned books by Malcolm X and Bobby Seale. *Time* reproduced the first quatrain, meticulously copied in a prisoner's neat script. Showing far less care, the magazine identified the words as "written by an unknown prisoner, crude but touching in its would-be heroic style." Two issues later, a concerned reader, "Gwendolyn Brooks of Chicago," corrected the error, rebuking *Time*'s "poetry specialist," who failed to recognize "one of the most famous poems ever written." Pointedly, Brooks concluded her letter by quoting the poem in full.

42. Mshaka's poem would later be republished in *Prison Writing in 20th-Century America*, ed. H. Bruce Franklin (London: Penguin, 1998), 178–79.

43. Thompson, *Blood in the Water*, 213.

44. LeRoi Jones (Imamu Amiri Baraka), *Black Music* (1968; New York: Da Capo, 1998), 196.

45. Shepp's concert is mentioned in Anthony Bannon, "Seeking a Revolution of Mind in Attica," *Buffalo Evening News*, September 16, 1972, B-9. The concert is also discussed in Peter Doggett, *There's a Riot Going On: Revolutionaries, Rock Stars, and the Rise and Fall of the 60s* (New York: Grove Press, 2009), 99. According to Doggett, "The Panthers' newspaper ignored the efforts of jazzman Archie Shepp to keep the plight of the widows and families of the Attica State casualties in the spotlight. . . . Shepp's finely crafted *Attica Blues* album received little notice, even after he played a concert at the institution on 4 July 1972."

46. For an important study of Black poets' textual experimentation during this period, see Aldon Lynn Nielsen, *Black Chant: Languages of African-American Postmodernism* (Cambridge: Cambridge University Press, 1997).

47. As mentioned earlier, Tisdale assigned Randall's *The Black Poets* as a textbook for his class. Baraka's "Black Art" is included in Randall's anthology, so Norris would certainly have had easy access to the poem.

48. William J. Harris, *The Poetry and Poetics of Amiri Baraka: The Jazz Aesthetic* (Columbia: University of Missouri Press, 1985), 75.

49. Amiri Baraka, *The Autobiography of LeRoi Jones* (New York: Freundlich, 1984), 187.

50. One exception is Lee Bernstein, *America Is the Prison: Arts and Politics in Prison in the 1970s* (Chapel Hill: University of North Carolina Press, 2010). For a recent critical study of Baraka, see James Smethurst, *Brick City Vanguard: Amiri Baraka, Black Music, Black Modernity* (Amherst: University of Massachusetts Press, 2020).

51. Norfolk Prison Brothers, ed., *Who Took the Weight? Black Voices from Norfolk Prison* (Boston: Little, Brown, 1972).

52. Elma Lewis, foreword to Norfolk Prison Brothers, *Who Took the Weight?*, xii.

53. Lewis, foreword, xv.

54. For other community-based poetry workshops in Black communities during this time, see, for example, Sonia Sanchez, ed., *Three Hundred and Sixty Degrees of Blackness Comin at You: An Anthology of the Sonia Sanchez Writers Workshop at Countee Cullen Library in Harlem* (New York: 5X Publishing, 1971).

55. Juno Bakali Tshombe / Craig Dee Anderson, "Attempt—or The Reason Why the Revolution / Is Getting Off to a Bad Start," in Norfolk Prison Brothers, *Who Took the Weight?*, 7. Cosmic or astral jazz albums released in 1972—the year Tisdale began his Attica workshop and *Who Took the Weight?* was published—include Pharoah Sanders's *Black Unity*, Alice Coltrane's *World Galaxy*, and Sun Ra's *The Night of the Purple Moon*, among many others.

56. Juno Bakali Tshombe / Craig Dee Anderson, "Psychological Warfare at Norfolk Prison Camp," in Norfolk Prison Brothers, *Who Took the Weight?*, 95.

57. Robin D. G. Kelley, *Freedom Dreams: The Black Radical Imagination* (Boston: Beacon, 2002), 6.

58. James, "Introduction," xxxii.

59. Readers might also look to Attica prisoner A. Jabar's poem "This iS A recording" in *The Last Stop: Writing from Comstock Prison*, ed. Joseph Bruchac (Greenfield Center, NY: Greenfield Review Press, 1974), 17–21.

60. For a history of the uprising and the post-uprising brutality told in graphic novel form, see Frank "Big Black" Smith, *Big Black: Stand at Attica* (Los Angeles: Archaia, 2020).

61. James, "Introduction," xxxii.

62. Harold E. Packwood, letter to Celes Tisdale, October 13, 1972, in Celes Tisdale's personal archive.

Introduction
to the Original Printing of *Betcha Ain't: Poems from Attica*

(Detroit: Broadside Press, 1974)

Celes Tisdale

I am not now, nor have I ever been, a prison inmate, so I realize that I cannot begin to comprehend the feelings of men without freedom. But, they touched me through their poems and taught me new meanings of freedom and dignity.

Attica Correctional Facility, formerly called Attica State Prison, is a maximum security symbol: maximum security since 1931, and, since September 1971, a symbol of what inhuman beings do to each other. Whatever the reasons or motivations for the disturbance at Attica during that week of September 9 through 13, 1971, the world knows, now, that all motivations were obliterated by the State's reaction of force which resulted in the death of thirty inmates and thirteen prison guards. The problems of prison reform and rehabilitation were once more focused upon as a major social problem of the twentieth century alleviated to a relatively small degree since the nineteenth century. Our writers workshop at Attica, out of which was born this book, was the result of Attica: September 9–13.

In the spring of 1972, as a rehabilitative measure for Attica, Hospital Audiences, Incorporated, contacted the Buffalo Black Drama Workshop's artistic director, Ed Smith, and Earl Sinclair, administrative director, relative to having the workshop sponsor a poetry workshop at Attica. Hospital Audiences, based in New York City, is a nonprofit organization one of whose purposes is to provide tickets for, transportation to, or entertainment within various institutions.

The New York State Council on the Arts provided other funds to buy books and defray the prison workshop director's expenses incurred in the weekly seventy-mile round trip by automobile from Buffalo to Attica. A small stipend was also provided. Buffalo's Model Cities Program was an indirect sponsor in that it subsidized the Black Drama Workshop.

Earl Sinclair recommended me as director of the Attica Workshop which was to be a kind of extension of the writers workshop I was conducting within the Black Drama Workshop. Randy Lerner, a coordinator with Hospital Audiences, made the arrangements with prison officials who established a lottery system of choosing fifteen different men for each series of eight-week sessions which began on May 24, 1972. At this writing, all funds have been cut for the program, but I still conduct sessions once a month instead of weekly.

From my first session with the men, their sensitivity and perception were so intense that each Wednesday night, I came away completely exhausted. Such a focusing of attention was required of me, but the men who developed as poets justified my presence there and gave themselves a kind of kinship with the universe.

Such a variety of poetic expression is found in the men's work. I expected otherwise, at first, in that it is assumed that incarcerated people will write mostly about their immediate situation and spout pat, rhetorical phrases. Interestingly, there was almost a total absence of that kind of poetry.

Harold Packwood's incisive wit in his "Red-Neck Coke Machine" is an almost dramatic show of versatility compared with his chilling "Night Flight to Hanoi." I mean, having to use the back of a Southern Coke machine is a rather interesting counterpoint to "Dress your children in Napalm colors / Arraying shrapnel-braided hair."

John Lee Norris asks the rhetorical question in his poetic statement: "Betcha Ain't." Have you ever seen an "aborigine smile," or "a Zulu chief / conjuring up / the bones of wisdom," or even "a tangerine sun / kiss / the rolling hills and / mountain valleys of Africa"?

Or, check out Chris Sutherland's "treatise" on Black women which begins:

I remember all your
Black bluesy moods
Of surprised, high-pitched laughter
And eye-rolling explosive anger
Your little moment of proud independence.

Brother Sanford X (Sanford Harris) describes himself as stoic. His terseness is summed up in his "Extremist," and his love for the teachings of the Honorable Elijah Muhammad is reflected in "A Humble Muslim."

And, among others, there is the elegance of haiku by Lewis Alexander Brooks, the pathos of Hersey Boyer, the truth of Jamail (Robert Sims), and the modern commentary of this society by Charles Johnson, which make this collection an experience. Maybe, it is true as Mshaka said in his "Formula for Attica Repeats": "They came / like so many unfeeling fingers / groping without touching / the 43 dead men / who listened / threatening to rise / again." Let's hope not.

The men challenged, "cracked" on me, "signified," and often disagreed with me. But, always, there was that respect that men establish among themselves. I kept a diary of my impressions of the men, their works, and the sessions. As you read their poems and excerpts from my diary, it is hoped that you will begin to know and love the men as I do, and understand what they meant during that week in September 1971, when they said, "We are men."

Betcha Ain't

Poems from Attica

(originally published by Dudley Randall's Broadside Press in Detroit, 1974)

Brother Amar

Forget?

They tell us to forget Golgotha we tread
   scourged with hate because we dared
to tell the truth of hell
   and how inhuman it is within.

The Autumn Song

It is here in the
Autumn of my times

That Spring's elusive splendor
Has become a common thing

And Summer's sweet enchanting
Magic
Has withered like a rose.

It is here in the
Autumn of my times
That I have found
The grace to sing

Speed

And now we see the light of yesterday
exploding a thousand triggertons upon the horizontal
vibrations of this still-born day.

And now we hear the heart beat
playing polyrhythms of life's sweet overture
ebbing ever so faintly into tranquility.

Then, unannounced, as a thief at your door
we mount the waves, descending slowly,
back to earth and home.

Attica Reflections

It isn't strange to awake in the silence
Of midnights,

To hear MEN weeping, in harsh and gravelly voices
That turn away your lies.

They have witnessed the slaughter
And heard your songs of merriment
As you filled your cups with blood.

Anoint yourselves in madness,
Dance with Hitler's ghost.

L. Alexander Brooks

Some Haiku

    The kiss of sunset
Soothes the innocent longing
    Of the blushing earth.

    Icicles melting,
Drip onto others beneath,
    Freeze, and are reborn.

    Susanna, dancing
Soars like the spray of fountains
    Kidnapped by the wind.

Dialing

Dialed a number: Got the time.
    (Hey, that's neat!)
Got the weather for a dime.
    (Well, you can beat . . . !)

They've got a number you can dial
    for the latest quotes
    on Quaker Oats
    (preferred or common,
    convertibles, warrants,
    and ex-dividends);

And the inning-by-inning Series scores,
And the speed at which traffic is moving,
So you can tell if the flow is improving

Well enough so that cars on the Expressway
Won't get ticketed for overtime parking;

And a number where a canned hostess announces
That at Kennedy, Newark, and LaGuardia,
Things have congested so in the last hour,
That after three hours' circling and bounces,
Flight 706 — already delayed seven hours
By bomb-threats and skyjacking rumors (not yet confirmed) —
Is being diverted by Providence *to* Providence
Where the field will shortly be completed.

Finally, there is a number — not listed —
Where the devout can dial God direct,
And tell him their troubles: ten cents for three minutes.
        But the line is always busy,
        Or the phone just keeps ringing and ringing,
        And nobody ever answers, not even Nobody;
And then, when, disgruntled, I hang up,
I never seem to get my dime back,
All of which makes me wonder,
        IS SOMEBODY TRYING TO TELL ME SOMETHING?

1st Page

They say our isolation is justifiable
So, when I'm released
I'll find a house or hut to live in
In a lonely countryside
   With Atticka on my mind.

Tears

If tears could destroy,
Our plight would cease.

Sleep

Come sleep
I dread this feeling
For life is so far ahead of me
And death just lingers . . .

People

People are very strange.
Do you know that an old, bald-headed lady
Ran two yards and jumped on my back
Whispered in my ear . . .
But, like I said,
People are very strange, you know.

Chico

To Moms
(For soul things they don't speak of)

When they speak of soul things,
They don't speak of drying young tears,
or holding young heads to breasts
like you used to do for me.

And they don't speak of soul love kisses
in between bandaging scraped elbows and knees.
And they don't speak of boogie man nights
or stormy, wintry days
when the only places I had to go
and the only friend I had was you.

And licking the bowl
and eating that last piece of chicken
that you knew Daddy wouldn't want.
Or giving me a bath and watching
while I swam to Africa
making sure I didn't drown.
Or, making sure I said my prayers
and tucking me in.

No, they don't speak of these soul things.

Bill Dabney

Cage Kill Label

Cage if he eats bananas
he must be a monkey
Cage if he sometimes growls
he must be a mad dog
Kill if his hair is long, afro,
he must be revolutionary, guerrilla
Kill black jacket and tam
blends with the night
defends people, right on,
Black Panther

Isaiah Hawkins

13th of Genocide

The clouds were low
   when the sun rose that day.
For the white folks were coming
   to lay some black brothers away.

From eight surrounding counties,
   the white folks came,
with 12 hundred locks
   and some brand new chains.

The word was kill niggers,
   kill all you can.
For they don't have the right
   to live like men.

Then up in the sky
   appeared a big green bird.
And from inside came
   these few words.

"Put your hands on your heads
   and you won't get hurt,
lie on your bellies,
   put your face in the dirt."

Then from a distance
   came a black brother's cry.
"I'm a man, white folks,
   and like a man I'll die."

Jamail (Robert Sims)

Dainty-Stepping Peaches

'Nuff said bout them
   Jive pimps.
Want to speak on them
   Fast hoes.
Dainty-stepping Peaches bought
   Five Cadillacs.
Four black.
Bitch gave a honkie one,
Then rounded on me:
"What I look like
Sitting in a tank,
   Nigger!"
'Nuff said?
'Nuff said—uh huh!

Brown-Eyed Devil

Allah is the best of knowers,
But the devil is hip too,
with his big old Afro.

Revolution Is

Black brother—
   revolution is loving you,—
for a change;
   calling you brother
instead of Mutha,—
for a change.
Even grinning at you—
   for a change.
Then—killing them,
   not you,—
for a change.

Buffalo

Buffalo is a drag town;
   I ran through it screaming.
I saw drugged drags nodding
   into oblivion,—dying as painlessly as vile odors.

I saw little girls in dirty sneakers
   faking it with lil-boys in dirty faces.
In the dark doorways where love is bargained for,
   I saw sis fornicating with the beast.
And my brothers locked-up like yogas
   with the daughters of Babylon.

I saw law and order prevailing there
   with its greedy hands extended.
Buffalo is a Roman family town with a
   Mafia-pizza morality, and it's a just wind that
   carries the stench of the ghetto to the critics on the hill.
Buffalo is a drag town—
   I ran through it screaming.

Pre-sentence Report

Dumb honkie called me an
"irresponsible para-military
black rabble rouser."
—Faggot European doctor
called me some dumb shit too,
lots of Latin nouns that
old Sigmund couldn't EVEN spell,
but I saw what they entered
in the court journal—
Bad Nigger—Watch him!

Quit Dreaming

Quit dreaming—
    original Asiatic blackman.
White boy ain't gonna
    let you build no nation
    in this land! Without a rumble.
Think about it.
Can't stop no tank
    with a bean pie.

The Cure

Feeling blue?
    Slap a honkie!
It's good therapy.
God's kindest
non-narcotic
panacea.

Jamal (Joseph Kitt)

Tempting

She was nutmeg brown with hair
    that blossomed like a cotton bush,
and her teeth were ivory rows,
her skin like a baby washed in
    the Mississippi
    and laid in the sun to dry.
She glowed like the morning star
    and moved like the black panther.
In the summer nite cool,
    she can be seen on any Harlem street,
    for she is a Black woman,
    and her name is Tempting.

Charles Johnson

Polarization

Feels cold.
     has fur,
         color white,
           must be
           european.

Today

Whites playing Jesus
Blacks playing White
Latins in quandary
U.F.O. in sight.

Nature

Black seeds cannot grow
in White Earth. Weeds will
be the fruit of labor . . .

Good Old Days

Turn in your "Right on's" and "Power to the Peoples."
Feel the beat of a Cracker's Club in tune to "we shall overcome."
Replace the Ready-to-die make-up kit with a grin.
Boy, happy days are here again!

A Thought

Shifting eyes, lies,
Crooked smile misleading joy
Convince us that blood does flow in pale, pale skin.
Wield power for the jackal pack
Which pulls the string upon your back.
Shape your mouth in honor
And your nose grows like branches on a dead tree
Growing, Growing, Growing.
I know all about the jive wood cutter
That hooked you up,
Milhous.

Harvey A. Marcelin

**Solidarity and/or the More
with the United Merrier**

No Nikki
I can't
Snuff a redneck

Not for you
Angela Yvonne
Not for Kathleen

I will not kill a hick
Nor a solitary pig
Or even a Ku Klux honky

But with you
With you
Sisters, let's

Ice them all.

Theodore McCain Jr.

Mahalia

Swing low, sweet chariot
When placidly amid her voice
Was that which said: "Lay us down to sleep
And pray the lord our soul to keep."

"Even me" was one of her cries,
And even we
Must one day die.
And if she die before she wake,
Pray the Lord her soul to take.

As she sang of love and God,
Remember Mahalia.
Her voice echoed around the world,
Singing songs of days of triumph.

Marvin McQueen

Running It

Brothers telling it like it is
Not — how it should be
Or supposed to be
Or — how we want it to be
But like it is
And it's like it is
Until we get it
The way we want it.

Mshaka (Willie Monroe)

Formula for Attica Repeats

. . . . . and when
the smoke cleared
they came aluminum paid
lovers
from Rock/The/Terrible,
refuser
of S.O.S. Collect Calls,
Executioner.

They came tearless
tremblers,
apologetic grin factories
that breathed Kool
smoke-rings
and state-prepared speeches.
They came
like so many unfeeling fingers
groping without touching
the 43 dead men
who listened . . .
threatening to rise
again. . . .

Betcha Ain't

Hey!
Betcha ain't
never seen a tangerine sun
kiss
the rolling hills and
mountain valleys of Africa

or?
raindrops tap dancing
on the leaves of tall trees
that hold
multicolored fruit of all sizes
and shapes?
Betcha ain't
never seen blueblackbrown
children
smiling the smile
of happiness and innocence

or?
the old wrinkled black hands
of
a Zulu chief
conjuring up
the bones of wisdom

or?
a panther
zig zagging across a green meadow
muscles rippling under a
black velvet coat?

Hey!
Betcha ain't
never seen heat waves
hopscotching
over honey-colored wheat fields

or?
the beauty
of a mobile home
made of sea ash!

or?
ancient writings on sacred
temples,
ivory carvings, golden sculptures,
storytellers in the
marketplace of Nairobi

Hey!
Betcha ain't
never seen a rainbow
caaas———caaade over the Nile

or?
Kikuyu warriors strong of back
silver-tipped spear
in hand
dodging through the bush
like black streak lightning

or?
black bejeweled queens
skin
like purple grapes
hairstyles
of naturalness
eyes
like sea pearls
black brown-tipped breasts
rich and full
of the milk of life?
Betcha ain't
never seen an aborigine smile

or?
a Masai death dance

or?
an Egyptian sand storm
swirl and twirl and dance
before
the eyes of the Sphinx?

Hey!
Betcha
Ain't

Just Another Page

(September 13, 1972)

A year later
And it's just another page
And the only thing they do right is wrong
And Attica is a maggot-minded black blood sucker
And the only thing they do right is wrong

And another page of history is written in black blood
And old black mamas pay taxes to buy guns that killed their sons
And the consequence of being free . . . is death
And your sympathy and tears always come too late
And the only thing they do right is wrong
　　　　　And it's just another page.

Harold E. Packwood

The Red-Neck Coke Machine

Riding through Alabama,
    Stopped for gas,
Kinda thirsty,
Eyed
        A big red coke machine.
Put a quarter in,
And pulled the handle, (down)
        Quarter came back,
        Along with a note,
            Saying,
"Sorry, you'll have to use
        The back of the machine."

Black Dolphin

When my life was young,
I dreamed
        Of pretty things—
Little brown girls
        With rainbow ribbons
hugging laughing braids
And I
    chased them
        for a kiss
Smelling
        their
just washed faces
Smiles floating
    like

          ivory soap
Or—
I was
    a cowboy
Yeah
a real
    cowboy
With a black silk shirt
    and silver guns
notches on
        my pearl handles
easy riding
on a huge black
        stallion
silver reins gleaming
    dancing
in the sunlight
And—
    Bang!
I'd off the dude
with
    the dimples
his gray eyes
rolling
        shut
the blood painting
    abstracts
on his white shirt
. . . . And—
Mama's cooking
    would wake me up
Old fryin' pan
        burnt black
        Sizzling
breakfast smells
Making my stomach sing

and
   I'd
poke a toe
for wool slippers
on the popsicle floor
Sleepily—
   to the kitchen
watching
   the brown magician
at the stove
   pulling hip goodies
from dancing pots
warm hands
   touching my face
teeth flashing
     a
love smile
And following
   the frying smoke
to the falling ceiling
   I knew
my dreams
    were dreams
But love
    and pancakes
eased the pain
   of reality
Putting my head
   to her bosom
hiding the fear
I smelled her sweetness
   And—
Black was my favorite color.

Out of Black Love

Out of Black Love,
So I was born,
From pouring salt-water,
Glistening on brown backs,
Lost in the ecstasy
Of a stolen moment of freedom.

Out of Black Love,
So I have lived,
Upon the shattered concrete streets,
Running in the maze
Of a bitter jungle.

Out of Black Love,
So I have traveled,
From ghetto to ghetto,
Searching in the darkness
Of one-room homes.

Out of Black Love,
So I have loved,
With every fiber of my being,
Crying in agony
For my wounds to heal.

Out of Black Love,
So I have been shamed,
For being black among colors galore,
Whispering the ancient lyrics
Of Ethiopian love songs.

Out of Black Love,
So I have fled,
From the pain of longing,

Dreaming the dreams
Of the hookah pipe.

Out of Black Love,
So I have been born again,
From the lashes upon my back,
Calling Brother,
Out of Black Love.

Haiku

Not knowing summer
How does Harlem perfume streets
With African scents?

Which to value more
A dead bird sweet to the tongue,
Or living brown hands?

If the moon did not
dance beneath the lynching tree
Would grass still paint spring?

Cinquain

Bye-bye
unconsciousness
done woke up now and there's
gonna be a mighty long time
      till sleep.

Potato Chip Song Lady

Potato chip song lady,
    With your salty soul,
Your golden brown body,
I watch your sensuous lips,

Saying,
"I bet you can't take just one!"

If you'd open your bag,
I'd gladly try;

Chew your kiss, and
    End your crisp ways.

Hop-Sing, Lesson No. 1

Standing in line,
At the Chinese Laundry,
I heard Hop-Sing say,
    To an ofay;

"Sorry—no tickee,
    No launlee!"

I turned to leave,
Didn't have my ticket.

"Where you go?"
Hop-Sing said.

    "Ain't got my ticket man!"

"That's all right," he said,
    "I know you dude!"
(I think he winked)

Little Girl

Little black girl,
I'll buy you ribbons for your hair,
Comb your bush when you're five
How pretty you'll look,

And everyone will know
You're my child.

Teach you Swahili,
The history of the East,
You'll know your Grandfathers were kings,
And will be again,
And everyone will say,
You're a black child.

Read you poetry,
And sing black songs,
To hear your laughter tinkle, —like the rippling Nile,
And everyone will know
You'll be a proud woman.

Lift you high in the air,
With strong black arms,
The billows of your skirt
Making rainbow circles beneath the sun,
And you'll know the meaning
Of a song for my Father.

But your Mama don't love me no more,
And your Daddy won't be me.
Still if I should see you,
I will smile and speak,
We will not be total strangers,
When we meet.

Night Flight to Hanoi

Awake
   Land of the burning children,
The cocks crow their chilling sound,
Steel bomb-bay mouths
   Spill death on your breakfast mats.

Dress your children in napalm colors
Arraying shrapnel-braided hair,
Little girl pig-tails singing songs,
Hushed by gaseous smoke/old before noon.
   The sky drones the death song.

Run
   In your flaming dress/bare feet so light upon the ground,
Snatch the little one and Run
The gamut of exodus road
   Trembling in the morning heat;
Hold him tight to choke the fear,
Evade the screaming steel/searing smoke
Shot from the bowels of the pale rapers of Suzy Wong.

Rest
   Beside the burning tree/and weep,
The tears streak your sooted-gold face,
Fall upon molten-pink young hands/Scream the angry flesh
   Until night ends the horror-day.

Sleep
   Land of the burning children,
Sing me an oriental lullaby/then
Search the charred rice fields—till he is found,
The youngest son of your mother;
Search upon the torn road
   Beneath the still smoking cart.

Forget
   The pain of scarred hands and wait
For light to see—light to find;
Rest before the cocks grow again,
Rest while the night-bird sings
      Hiroshima Blues.

What Makes a Man Free?

What makes a man free?
Brass keys, a new court
Decision, a paper signed
By the old jail keeper?
What makes a man free?
A green dashiki, afroed
Down, way down,
Alligators snapping?
What makes a man free?
The need to be or the
Right to be, — the word
Uhuru! Uhuru! Uhuru!
What makes a man free?
Impressive words, implementation
Of social science,
The die-hard look?
What makes a man free?
Unchained mind-power and
Control of self—Freedom now!
Freedom now! Freedom now!

Sanford X

Extremist!

Extremist
Damn right
Caught extreme hell
take extreme action
bring extreme change
in extreme society

Guess Who

Speaks of P-E-A-C-E
Means P-I-E-C-E
Pale Face
Thin Skin
Blue Eyes
Murderer
Rapist
Liar
Base
Vagabond in the land
Hated by nations of the earth

Ain't It the Truth

Land of free white man
Home of bewildered,
Enslaved misused and abused Indian.
America the beautiful.

A Humble Muslim

Though I try to be but a humble Muslim
some say stoic and apathetic
my knowledge, wisdom, and understanding
have become my wealth.
I asked Allah for strength
that I might achieve;
I was made weak, that I might
learn humbly to obey.
I asked for health
that I might do great works;
I was given infirmity,
that I might do even better things.

I asked for riches;
I was given poverty
that I might become wise.
I asked for power;
I was given weakness, that I might feel the
need of Allah and His messenger.
I asked for all things that I might enjoy life;
I was given life that I might enjoy all things;
I got nothing that I asked for,
but got everything I needed.
Despite my selfishness, only unspoken prayers were answered.
I am among the most beautiful of black brothers—
all so richly blessed.

Allah U Akbar

Christopher Sutherland

At Last

At last—
No roaches.
Paint don't peel no more.
"Hit's" mighty cold,
but silent
'cause the rats don't roam the floor.
No worries 'bout no burglars
comin' thew the windows
or kickin' down the door.
No more pissy hallways
or junkies lurkin' roun'.
I 'vacuated the building
and burnt the motherfucker down!

Age

The old dream sweet words
that harmonize with blackeyed susans and
daffodils which strum their minds
on delicate spider webs
waking sleeping, weeping willows
whose fingers touch sweet earth
which holds our frozen cask.
The old singer does not sing but sobs
unheard by youth who laugh at silver tears
and run wildly, drunk with their golden age.
Spilling their comic brains,
they run, they run home
to suck the teat that heals

life's first stinging blow.
And when hairs grow sparse and gray
and our little circle of time begins to close,
we smile to our lonely selves and say
"That, used to be me."

Black Women!!

I remember all your
Black bluesy moods
Of surprised, high-pitched laughter
And eye-rolling explosive anger
Your little moment of proud independence
Cinnamon
Nut brown
Black sugar woman
That smiles
With a voice that speaks
In tones
Of sparkling eyes
That touch the heart
And bless the soul
With love—

Sept. 13

Let the drums roll
Give the first command
That puts us in the ground

    R - E - A - D - Y !

We stiffen our shoulders
Hold our heads up high
Let the world take note
That proud, black men
Are here about to die

66

    A-A-A-I-M !

If our actions
Cause brothers and sisters to unite
As we die,
In their fighting spirits we live.
So let the drums roll
And damn that final order that puts us in
The ground . . .

    F-I-R-E !

Was It Necessary?

Was it really necessary?
Did they really have to carry
Rifles and shotguns?
        Let's ask the gov',
        Who's so full of love!

Was it really necessary?
Did they really have to carry
Rifles and shotguns?
Against sticks and knives!
Was it worth 43 lives?
        Let's ask the gov',
        Who's so full of love!

Was it really necessary?
Did they really have to carry
Rifles and shotguns?
Shoot them with intent to kill!
Shoot them even when they lay still!
        Let's ask the gov',
        Who's so full of love!

Was it really necessary?
Did they really have to carry
Rifles and shotguns?
While troopers were killing with hate and glee,
Rock was safe in Albany!
        Wasn't he?

Let's ask the gov',
Who's so full of love!

Was it really necessary?
Did they really have to carry
Rifles and shotguns?
Rock on T.V., says he didn't know,
While 43 are helping daisies to grow!!
   Does it sound like I'm angry?
   Damn right, my heart pains me!!
     Let me tell you something
     Since it's time for me to split.
     Don't ask the governor nothing, Man,
     Cause he's full of it.
        Peace

Poet

    If I were a poet I would write a poem of love and
happiness and tell the world of my discovery.
If I were a poet.

Celes Tisdale's
Attica Poem and Journal

The Men

For you, the men,
    is given a place to be
    to think, to do what
    they would say is you.

But, you, the men,
    are of a Blacker mold
    that white cannot wash.

And, you, the men,
    are ever tuned to that
    among you/us which
    seeks to say and touch
    that which will destroy
      the "us" in you.

And, I came to lift,
    to tell, to read the world in poems,
    and paused in wonder
    at the men who really know.

**Attica—A Diary
(From the Outside/Inside)**

May 24, 1972

4:30 p.m. "Anticipation"

Many times have I basked in the glory of applause, adulation, recognition as I interpreted the Black poet masters. But, today, I wait in painful/joyful anticipation of meeting those humanity-scarred men who must express themselves or perish from anonymity.

Sitting here on my front porch waiting for Randy to pick me up, I suddenly realize that I have never sat on my front porch before. What enjoying faces on the buses! I really see their faces and talk with my neighbor next door for the first time. He offered to let me use his wax for my car. Can this heightening of perception of my surroundings be conscious preparation for what I'll be doing later today and every Wednesday for 16 weeks 6:00–9:00 p.m.? Can you imagine conducting, possibly, the first Black Poetry workshop inside a prison (maximum security). Maybe I'm making history—maybe.

Well, here's Randy in his green Volks somehow very much like himself: frantic, intense, a constant gear shift. He's Jewish.

5:30 p.m. "Before the Great Wall"

The air is hot, still, restless. Here, after an hour's ride exchanging philosophies and expectation. A front gate guard recognizes me, he says, and we exchange pleasantries (?) while waiting to be cleared to enter the inner walls. Randy does most of the talking. My mind is too full.

6:00 p.m. "Within"

Having passed all the doors, gates, guards, and serene atmosphere of the cool passageways, we arrive in the teaching area of "C" Block. I feel like the new schoolmarm in a one-room schoolhouse on the first day and I remember when I first faced a classroom nine years ago.

6:15 p.m.

The men are coming in now. I recognize some of them from the old days in Willert Park Projects and Smitty's restaurant where I worked during the undergraduate days. They seem happy to see me but are properly restrained (strained?).

May 25, 1972

Our first session was spent getting acquainted with each other. The following are some of the responses to my asking what is poetry: Personal, deals with emotions, historical, compact (concise), eternal, revolutionary, beauty, rhyme, rhythm, a verbal X-ray of the soul.

June 7, 1972

Angela Yvonne Davis was found innocent of all charges in California, and her trial was the topic of interest at the beginning of the session. Rather than become involved in a political discussion, I read a poem given to me by Nikki Giovanni called "Poem of Angela Yvonne Davis." It brought a warm response from the group.

July 5, 1972

Tonight there was much excitement among the workshop members. They were more talkative than usual and very excited about the recent (July 4) concert presented at the facility by Archie Shepp, Black jazz musician. We discussed the concert at length, because we felt that Black mu-

CELES TISDALE

sic is poetry and poetry is music. Christopher Sutherland (an inmate) presented a poem to the group which was a tribute to Archie Shepp.

It has been six weeks (sessions) now since we started the poetry workshop. We had no session last week (6/28) because of an entertainment group's performance at the facility and my being involved in a play: *Angela*. I haven't seen the men for two weeks and I notice today that the ranks have been somewhat decimated. In group I only ten men showed up, two of whom were new. The high interest level has been sustained.

I've been reading their works at home for the past three or four weeks and I'm very pleased at their poetry and have noticed a real flair for poetry among a number of the men: Boyer, "Point," Phillips, Sutherland, Dabney, Mackey, Bryant, Sanford X, to name a few. I plan to recommend their return in the next eight-week session.

"Sonny" Walker said Hawkins has been paroled—joy. Much excitement tonite over a poem in the text: "Giles Johnson, Ph.D." by Frank Marshall Davis.

The men are friendlier now and much more relaxed—even the reticent ones are budding, opening up, flowering. Received a compliment today, probably the most sincere ever: the brother privately told me that I was a fine example of Black intelligence and that I related well to them. They seem proud to know me and try to please, but do not fawn. I hope they know how proud I am of them. Everyone very talkative, almost festive mood. They did most of the talking and reading poetry (their own) while I tape-recorded it.

The men joke with me as we enter and leave, but I still detect great respect, almost awe, a stand-offish attitude. I see them as the men I relate to every day in the world outside. How it pains me when they go back to their cells, but linger and talk before the guard hurries them along. If I could only stay here a few days more.

July 12, 1972

Felt the anger, frustration, hostility of the men, firsthand tonite. I had secured adequate clearance for the Buffalo Black Writers Workshop to sit in on the session tonite, but Supt. Montanye canceled their coming, by a phone call to Randy, yesterday. I was apprehensive about telling the men of the cancellation, and they were most indignant about this broken promise, one of many, according to them. Feel a strong undercurrent of resentment for the administration. Am convinced that another riot is in the making. About 1/2 of the session was spent explaining the function of Hospital Audiences, and my role as a liaison with the administration. Most of the men insist that no change has taken place in the prison since the September incident.

Found out later in the session why the Buffalo Black Writers Workshop were not allowed in tonite. It seems some small demonstration took place yesterday by the inmates (hunger strike).

The men continue to produce, and some have really improved. A real pleasure to see growth. Next week, final evaluations and summaries.

July 20, 1972

Our workshop session was canceled yesterday because of Supt. Montanye's declaration of a state of emergency at the facility. Prisoners (approx. 900 of 1,200) have stayed in their cells the past two days protesting conditions. A specific protest centered around a nurse's termination. She was reinstated amid the protests.

When we resume 7/26, it will be our evaluative concluding session for the first eight weeks. Have gathered much poetry from the inmates—they want to publish a book—we'll talk about it later.

Randy very apprehensive about returning to facility—many prisoners' protests continue.

July 23, 1972

State of emergency has been lifted by Supt. Montanye. Prisoners (about 900) were in voluntary lock-in for three days.

One of my students, Robert Aldridge, wrote to me today: "I want to thank you for letting me participate in the poet's class," he says, "because it was very helpful in rehabilitating me and helping me to express my personal feelings in poems."

Arrived in Detroit last evening on way to Tisdale family reunion in Albion, Michigan. Staying at Verna Moore's house in Detroit suburb of Inkster. Mrs. Moore insisted we stay overnight and return tonite after leaving Albion. We had planned to stay in a motel. Verna is a very gracious and kind lady.

Dudley Randall invited me to his home last night in Detroit (20 miles away). We talked about poetry and publishing, naturally. He is a very well-read man and quite talkative. Much shorter and lighter complexion than when I first met him two years ago at Canisius College. And to think that the owner of the largest Black publishing firm in the U.S. would invite me to his home.

Mr. Randall, during our 1-1/2 hour visit together (9:00–10:30 p.m.), taught me so much about my poetry and the mechanics of publishing. He was especially interested in my Japanese Haiku and made good suggestions as to how I could improve. He also expressed great interest in our writers workshop in Buffalo, and our forthcoming publication, *We Be Poetin*. My workshop at Attica was of great interest to him, also. I intend to bring copies of *We Be Poetin* and the inmates' work back to Detroit in about three weeks for Mr. Randall's criticism.

Packwood told me about his idea for a Black education program that he thought would be acceptable to Attica's administration. His program would include Black History, Creative Writing, Language, Political Science, and especially land-based Economics. Packwood thought this might be frowned upon if practiced on a mass scale. "If I can say freedom in four Black languages," he told me, "then I am a 'violent revolutionary.'"

August 9, 1972

New eight-week poetry session began tonite. Group I consists of 15 returnees and Group II (11 men tonite) comprised mostly of Black Muslims. Some recognized me—many have strong political consciousness. Talking very spirited in both groups. Much concern about white inmate beaten by guards in the yard, today. Most expressed doubts about the brutality of Attica ever changing—most informative viewpoints. Haven't seen Randy for last two sessions.

August 16, 1972

Much relaxation and joking, free conversation in Group I tonite. Group I comprised of 15 returnees from first eight-week session.

Discussed my pending press conference 8/17/72 and the group approved after many questions about the press conference. Greatest concern of group was press interpretation and inclusion of all Black press.

My lecture on history of Black literature received enthusiastically amid much questioning. Abraham and Sanford X much learned in African and Muslim history—contributed well to discussion. Found that my choice of words under careful scrutiny by many who engendered discussion on what amounted to semantics.

Hersey Boyer, one of my best, missing tonite—in lock up—I was told he was "bitten by a dog," meaning the guards beat him up, I suppose. No one wanted to discuss it with the guard present in the room. How interesting—the guard sat in the room with us tonite—most unusual.

Group II liked Nikki Giovanni's "Ego Tripping" that I read to them and asked for copies. Much interest but not much writing ability in Group II—Mshaka Giza a standout, however.

Really a chuckle about my photograph—they thought the serious shot looked like a mugshot. It's supposed to be used for press release, ha!

The men really like what we're doing although only three in Group II show any real poetic potential.

August 25, 1972

At our last workshop meeting, Wednesday 8/23, discovered that Black guard had been assigned to us: John Hardy. We discussed philosophy of poetry in Group I (advanced) and began to see how very critical I am in evaluating poetry of the men. Some of them seem to be slacking off in production. Maybe they are preoccupied with other things. They are very interested in compiling enough poetry for a book. I am trying to minimize the importance of such at this point.

Buffalo Evening News wants to do feature story, but I refuse unless a Black reporter on the scene. The men concurred. Tony Bannon of *BEN* agreed to send Bill Watkins (Black reporter) with me to Attica and a white photographer.

August 30, 1972

We discussed proposed story in *Buffalo Evening News* during week of Sept. 13th one year after the riots. I asked their opinions and permission to have photographers and reporters come into the prison. We agreed to have only a Black photographer and reporter on the scene. We spent the entire first session discussing pros and cons of such a report's point of view. After more than an hour of discussing, we voted to allow a release of the story.

A bit disturbed about the small amount of poetry being produced lately. Qué pasa??

September 18, 1972

Big one-page spread in *Buffalo Evening News* this past Saturday, 9/16, on my activities in the Attica poetry workshop, written very well by Anthony Bannon. Much positive reaction to story and feel like a celebrity (smile).

A white man came by the house this evening. His name was Bill Jenkins. He had seen the article in the paper Saturday and said that he was very impressed with what I was doing. He gave me about ten books of poems he had collected. Among those books were: *Color*, by Countee Cullen (his first book, 1925); *Copper Sun*, by Countee Cullen, 1925, which was autographed by him; *God's Trombones*, by James Weldon Johnson, 1927 (fourth printing 1929); and *Lyrics of Lowly Life*, by Paul Laurence Dunbar, 1896, the 1908 edition. I believe the two by Cullen are first editions or close to it. Mr. Jenkins gave me the books, complimented me again, and left. Strange.

Met J. E. Gaines (Sonny Jim), playwright from New Lafayette Theatre, tonite. Interesting person. Has play just closed off-Broadway: "Sometimes a Hard Head makes a Soft Behind." He's in his middle forties. His youngest daughter was born on the same day as my son, Eric, 5/21/72.

September 20, 1972

After two-week layoff, got together tonite, discussed the article with Group I for criticism. Favorable reactions to it. Sanford X dissented, but I expect him to want the last word.

Interesting—the guard, John Hardy, who is Black, mentioned to me afterwards that the men never thought to thank me for my efforts. He said that they don't realize that you can only do so much for them—they often don't appear to appreciate things or favors. He made me think.

September 27, 1972

Just arrived home from Attica—very tired—but elated over especially good responsive night among the men. Group I, "the pros," wanted to know the mechanics of playwriting and I spent most of the hour explaining how to write a play. Many good questions engendered. The editor of the Attica newspaper sat in. He is a white inmate. He appeared entertained and took many notes.

Group II requested copies of Nikki Giovanni's "Ego Tripping" and passed out copies tonite. They also requested the lyrics of "Superfly" by

Curtis Mayfield which I taped and played for them. Some members show good promise, but many still not contributing.

October 11, 1972

Very good session tonite, after last week's cancellation (I was exhausted). Only Group I present because of another administrative mix-up.

Tape-recorded everyone reading his poems or poem from book. The men genuinely concerned about my illness last week. Sutherland sent me a card. "Point" (Harold Packwood) may be released in January with Mr. Stillwell's (his friend) and my help. We have arranged for his getting into college.

I visited an inmate's wife here in Buffalo upon his request. She was not very encouraged by the prospect of his parole. I suppose there was much tension between them because of his "habit." She appeared to be living fairly "fast" herself.

We made (workshop) plans for the publication of our book of poems. I plan to contact Dudley Randall in Detroit after our last session, on 10/18/72. We shall not begin a new session until 12/6/72 because of my playing in *The Fantasticks* during November.

October 19, 1972

Tonite, Eric Daughtry and James Allen went with me to Attica, and both groups met together for a reading-rap session.

Bill Dickinson and another white person also sat in, as did a white guard with our regular Black guard. Although Dickinson is director of education and special programs, he is not appreciated by the men, generally. I guess it's understandable—his position and all.

Session was quite tense until Dickinson left. The other white was a prison inmate and editor of the newspaper. Eric and James provided an interesting dimension thru reading their poems and talking about our writers workshop. James was home on leave from the Navy. I read some of my poems, too.

Generally, the session was very spirited with almost everyone reading his poems. The men really appreciated the contact with other men from the world outside. The men were so inspired to continue the workshop during my absence for the month of November.

Received a note from another inmate not in our class: Daudi, who taught me Swahili on the outside. He requested that I try to recover the books used from Ed Lawrence at the African Cultural Center.

Abraham (an Ethiopian Jew) has really blossomed and was the hit of the session this evening. He confided to me that he really enjoyed Anita Cabrera's poems in our book. He gave me a note to give to her expressing his admiration. I was reluctant in that it may be a precedent, but since she is a member of our Black Writers Workshop in Buffalo, I didn't think any real harm could be done.

October 31, 1972

The inmates (workshop) and administration invited me to an appreciation reception, today 1:00–3:30 p.m. Surprised to see men sitting in chairs in reception bldg; very quiet. Coffee and coke had not arrived when I appeared at 1:30. Usual bureaucratic hold-up I suppose.

Noticed the uniform of the guards has changed—they wear blazers and gray slacks. Must admit they look less oppressive.

Men were sitting so formally, I felt need to walk around speaking to each little group. They loosened up after I talked briefly about poetic directions to the entire group. However, it appeared that the men wanted to discuss political directions and the American system. After about 15 minutes of such discussion, I steered back to poetry discussion.

Surprised to see coffee in large pots and to find the cake tasted a bit coarse, like old home recipe. Dickinson told the group they could meet during the month of November but stipulated that political discussion must be curtailed. Frankly, I agree with him. The men promised me that they would have a play ready when I see them again, Dec. 6, 1972, for the start of the new, third 16-week session.

Couldn't figure out why Harold Packwood was not present at the reception. He organized it and is the standout in the workshop. Someone mentioned that he was practicing on his saxophone.

It appears that the men have greater perception of their existence and are much more concerned now with all aspects of writing. Such respect that they show me I have never known. Fantastic!

November 3, 1972

Received a letter from Chris Sutherland (Attica) expressing his appreciation how I helped him as a poet and a person. He is the only person who seems really concerned about my inner thoughts and feelings.

November 4, 1972

Received letter from Packwood (Attica) in which he explained the reason for his absence from the reception on Tues., 10/31. He was rehearsing on his sax for the Black Awareness Day to be held at the prison on 11/6/72 at 9:00 a.m. Dickinson called me the other day to participate. I suspect I will, but not as a celebrity. I should rather watch and have a minimum amount of input.

December 6, 1972

Arrived tonite to find there was no scheduled workshop session—another foul-up by Dickinson. Stayed to watch movie scheduled and learned much about Persia. (ha!)

Packwood's parole denied—a friend of his called to tell me. Next Board, Feb. 1974.

December 13, 1972

Met the men tonite after a five-week layoff. Packwood very despondent—I'm afraid of the negative effect of a denied parole. Chris Sutherland also very despondent because authorities confiscated much of his work.

Most of the evening spent talking about poets, especially Nikki Giovanni. Generally, the men feel that her popularity has made her ego trip.

They really "come down" hard on her. Their biggest objection was to her seemingly having to explain her actions if they seem contrary to the norm. I suggested that I would bring a taped recording of her reading to next week's session.

The remainder of the evening was spent reading original poems. The men were most eager to read and very enthusiastic. I showed them the manuscript that Ann, Beverly, and I had completed and I read some poems from it.

December 17, 1972

Packwood says he's been suffering from "growing pains" in his writing. "I'm beginning to feel my growth as a Black writer," he tells me, "and constantly seeking new modes of expression." His thoughts, he says, "are just popping up from everywhere" and he's now developing the habit of writing these thoughts down.

December 20, 1972

Tonite, we began our first two-hour session. From now on, we intend to meet 6:30–8:30 with both groups combined. More time.

I switched the tape to Imamu Amiri Baraka (LeRoi Jones) 4/72 and his comments provided discussion for the entire evening.

The men have become quite sophisticated in their poetic tastes and versatility. Their criticism of poems and poets is most perceptive. We really got into quite a discussion as to what constitutes a poem, and what Blacks should be writing about, today. Most of them agree that our work should reflect the times. Chris, Abraham, and Thurman were concerned that we not lose a wide range, and Chris stressed the need for exercising the imagination more often as poets. How profound and mature!

Marv McQueen is coming home on furlough Saturday. He is staying around the corner from us. I'll see him during the holidays.

A most interesting point came up tonite. I asked why Black poets do not seem to write humorous poems these days too often. The men said (some of them) that Black people have nothing to be happy about. When

I told them that I am constantly happy, they agreed, but found it hard to believe. Strange!

December 27, 1972

Tonite, we began with one of Imamu's earlier tapes I made (4/70). The purpose was to compare his tone in this speech with the one we heard last week from 4/72. We especially noted his poems on the recording.

Since we began this poetry workshop May 24th I have noticed how increasingly reflective and philosophical a number of the men have become. Many of them have begun to use language well in poetry and very interested in the power of the word. With this in mind, I began talking about Japanese haiku poetry and taught them how to write it. With haiku, the poet must write a poem comprised of only 17 syllables. I am eager to see what they will do by next week.

January 3, 1973

A new year—great optimistic feeling. But that's not new—I feel this way almost every day I wake up.

Played tape recording of Don L. Lee. Men enjoyed his poetry.

We continued our discussion of haiku and read our own haiku. The men were quite good. Jamail was especially good. He appears to be well learned and is the Imam in a Muslim sect. Haiku is a natural for him. Abraham (Brathwaite) finally found a poetic medium. Packwood, surprisingly, did not do well with haiku.

January 10, 1973

More talk about haiku tonite. Only nine men present tonite. I supposed they were involved in other activities or working. Chris Sutherland, one of our best, was missing. I am very concerned about him. He seems unusually despondent these days. His cell was "raided" by officials and his poetry and books confiscated. He has been very tight, recently.

Packwood recovering from his shock of denied parole. He seems more cheerful, now. Ed Stillwell, an influential man in the prison, came to see him this week. An appeal to the parole is forthcoming.

Introduced the cinquain as a poetic form tonite. We'll see what next week brings.

Abraham and Thurman Williams have been paroled—Great!

January 17, 1973

Spent the evening in poetic analysis of established poems that I passed to group. Many quite perceptive, especially with "No Images" by Waring Cuney. We spent half the time talking about our own poetry. Pleased to notice great improvement in many of the men and to see Joe Hardy writing again. Chris Sutherland returned after one-week absence. Don L. Lee wrote him a letter.

Interesting tonite in that some of the men very restless and talkative while others trying to express selves. Very annoying.

January 24, 1973

Only nine men present tonite, but time well spent. It seems there are so many programs going on as well as metal shop for which the men are paid. I suppose many of the workshop members can't always get away on Wednesday nites for the workshop.

We spent more time in analysis of three literary pieces: the poem "Soul" by Barbara Simmons; an excerpt from Pulitzer Prize (1970)–winning Black play, *No Place to Be Somebody* by Charles Gordone, "They's mo' to being Black"; and a one-character play, *On the Road* by Tony Preston.

As usual, the men showed fine perception offering insights that my college classes never touched upon. Of course, these men have more life experiences, generally, from which to draw. We plan to continue analyzing the three pieces, next week.

Chris Sutherland received more mail from Don L. Lee as well as books and magazines. I am happy I made that contact possible for Chris.

January 31, 1973

Completed last session of eight-week period tonite. Group very responsive to activities tonite: analyzing three literary pieces (see 1/24/73). Plan to seek publication of poetry while taking off for the month of February. Going to Detroit to seek out Dudley Randall of Broadside Press. If not successful, will go to white publisher (Bantam).

At this point, I feel we have enough poems to make a very substantial book. I also feel that the uniqueness of the project will sell itself. How I wish I succeed in publishing this most important testament of man's creative bent!

March 14, 1973

New, and maybe last eight-week session began tonite. It may be the last sessions in that funds for the Black Drama have been completely cut effective 8/1/73. New York State Council on the Arts provides much of our support and may bail this program out.

Only three men present, two of whom were new. Very discouraging to see administrative laxity in getting the men together. I left a note for Dickinson about the situation.

Had a good session, though. We used the "Psycho-Gram," renamed the "Tis-O-Gram" in recognition of my having created it [see appendix]. It deals with providing concrete forms in writing for abstract ideas. The two guards were so interested that they joined in the exercise. The Black guard, a new one, asked me for a copy of *Harlem Gallery* by Melvin B. Tolson. I promised to bring it next week.

March 28, 1973

Interesting session in that we got into specific mechanics of poetry, especially the uses of haiku. Specific examples were taken from some of the former members of the workshop and *We Be Poetin!*

Played tape of Don L. Lee recorded 4/71. His philosophy examined, and next week, we shall hear his poetry.

Good vibes in class tonite. Men very talkative and many shared their poems. We have talked much more about poetic technique than ever before. The men absorb almost everything. Intended to play speech by Imamu Baraka (recorded 3/30/73) but time allowed only 15 minutes.

I think the most important point I made tonight was that we must not judge a poet by what he "seems" to be or has become, because the poet's approach often changes to fit the occasion or prevailing social/political tenor of the society: he (poet) is so elusive. One workshop member cautioned us that we should not judge people like Imamu or Nikki Giovanni by their past (white wife of Imamu and Goldwater supporting Nikki). We must recognize transitions. How honest the transitions is a matter of pure (impure?) conjecture.

We talked about what poetry is supposed to do to or for the reader or listener. The men thought poetry should teach, entertain, and most of all be an outer expression of inner impressions. Poetry is reflective and impressionistic perhaps?

Interestingly, I am beginning to define and distill my reactions to poetry and its purpose. Just as the men, I am still learning/formulating. As Packwood said tonite: "The only constant thing is change."

Most of the session was spent listening to each other's poetry and criticizing it. The writers were asked to explain their work before being evaluated as to their technique. My greatest concern now is that more men need to contribute their work. Sanford X particularly troubles me in that he is such a precise thinker and critic, but he has not written anything in months.

Returned poetry written last week. "Chico" especially stood out, and Hersey Boyer continued to produce. Still, only one-half of 20 men are producing.

Spent time, also, discussing typical errors in beginning poets and how to rectify them. Stressed objection to superfluity and cliché. Really felt learning taking place.

June 2, 1973

Packwood has been transferred to Albion Correctional Facility in Albion, New York, a small town between Buffalo and Rochester. He can't believe there aren't any locks! He wants me to write him a letter of recommendation to Buffalo State College. Albion will let him go to classes during the day and return to the prison at night. He would be a student in the English Department in Assemblyman Arthur Eve's SEEK Program (Seek Education Enlightenment Knowledge).

June 6, 1973

Returning to Attica today after one-month layoff to do *Hurricane Season* and T. S. Eliot's *Cocktail Party*. The roles were most successful, especially Dr. Reilly in Eliot's play. I believe that was the high point of my career. As I write this, I am sitting in a gas station at Sycamore and Fillmore where I usually fill up on my way to Attica—will continue later, tonite, after the session.

. . . Session had small attendance tonite. Many thought I was not coming and no one had been informed about my taking off for a month. Another communications breakdown. The men were certain that prison officials purposely did not inform them. Well, anyway, we discussed the acceptance of the book for publication. Great happiness and anticipation. Some of the men will write to the publisher, Dudley Randall, thanking him and Broadside Press. Really pleased that we chose a Black publisher or that they chose us. Next week, we shall appoint an executive committee to decide how funds will be handled from book sales. Title will be *Betcha Ain't* taken from one of Lee Norris's poems.

We discussed little poetry tonite and spent time listening to original poems on tape being read by fifth- and sixth-grade Black schoolchildren at schools 48, 37, and 12. I have been working with them during the last week in cooperation with members of the Buffalo Philharmonic Orchestra and Young Audiences. Dynamite kids!

Found that more men have been transferred or released: Lee Norris, Packwood to Albion, McQueen to Albion. Received letter from Packwood in Albion. He's enjoying it. Strange!

Good sessions although only five men present. The others were enjoying yard privileges tonite until 9:30.

We discussed poetry variations as shown on a taped recording of Ossie Davis and Ruby Dee. They were doing readings in African oral tradition, poems by Bob Kaufmann, and poems from a book edited by Ruby Dee called *Glow Child* which contained poems by unknown young Blacks. The men thoroughly enjoyed the tape, but more importantly, they were able to hear different forms read than the usual Don L. Lee, Baraka, Sanchez, or Giovanni. Again, we realized the great diversity in Black poetry.

Also, told the men of phone conversation I had today with New York City and Miss Barbara Slantz of New York State Council on the Arts who has heard of our program and intends to seek further funding after we terminate 6/27/73.

Anthony Bannon called today and wants to do a follow-up feature story on the Attica workshop and the book. Tomorrow, he will have a preliminary announcement in the *Buffalo Evening News*.

June 25, 1973

Visited Albion Community Preparation Center in Albion, N.Y., to see brother-in-law, Ronnie Parker, and member of Attica workshop, Harold Packwood. Ronnie and Packwood have been transferred here from Green Haven and Attica, respectively, during the past month. I understand this is the "last leg" of a prison sentence.

No walls at Albion and atmosphere quite free. Inmates and guests are allowed to walk around the grounds. Ronnie humorous as usual and Packwood eager as ever to "hit the streets." Played a little basketball with another inmate.

Met two other brothers from Attica workshop: Marvin McQueen and "Chico." I reported on the book much to their pleasure.

June 26, 1973

Tony Bannon and Jim Pappas have been cleared to accompany me tonite to Attica to do on-the-scene report. Jim will do the photography for the *Buffalo Evening News* story. The inmates' reactions and tone of discussion should prove interesting.

Last Wednesday (6/20) we finalized plans in workshop for establishing a special fund for royalties from the book. The majority requested that the royalties be put into a Black bank, preferably the Bank of Islam (Elijah Muhammad) in Chicago. I am rather dubious about the funds being kept so far away and the possible "political" implications of such a move. I told the men I shall investigate the possibility.

June 28, 1973

Spent interesting two hours with Tony Bannon at *Buffalo Evening News* working out details for story on the workshop and book of Attica. He wants to use excerpts from this diary and letters from Packwood. Sounds interesting. He liked the diary, but most excited about the letters which, he said, would make an interesting book.

Bannon is planning to release the story to any national publication that is interested: *Ebony*, *Saturday Review*, *Ramparts*, etc. Interesting—he had three of his own poems accepted by *Poetry* magazine.

June 29, 1973

Chris Sutherland, former Attica inmate and workshop member, called from N.Y.C. tonite. He seems to be doing all right since he's been out: '73 Cadillac, a woman, and a job.

June 30, 1973

Have received Attica manuscript from Mr. Randall at Broadside. He kept 25 poems he especially liked and returned 100 poems to me for revision and my suggestions. I shall send new poems and revised ones back to him in about two weeks. Such a chore to insure success of the project. But, encouraging to receive definite layout of royalties and other particulars from Broadside Press. Stayed up until 2:30 yesterday morning revising, editing, and rejecting poems for the collection which, I am sure, will be a success with the right publicity angles. I'll handle publicity in the Western New York area.

August 1, 1973

Returned to Attica after one-month hiatus. Only five men present for this session. Program not funded yet for this eight-week session. Have not heard from N.Y.S. Council on Arts. A new education director, Mr. Salay, assured me of new and better communication—ha! Session very good, though.

We listened to Nikki Giovanni's new recording, *Like a Ripple on a Pond*, on which she reads poetry to the backing of a gospel choir. We agreed that much of the poetry does not fit the gospel songs and that the recording, as her previous one, *Truth Is on Its Way*, is largely commercial.

During the session, we listened to and evaluated each other's poetry. The men really want to hear their own previous discussions on tape. Next week, I shall comply and also get back into teaching more. An inmate named Luster stopped me in the hall and asked to join us. I shall see what I can do.

August 6, 1973

Settled matter of Packwood getting out of Albion to be on T.V. show I am moderating to be telecast 8/12/73 (Sun) 10:30 CBS. A minor miracle.

CELES TISDALE

Apparently, Packwood's all set for Buffalo State, and he's excited to continue his writing there. I'd written him a long letter of recommendation for the program. As Packwood says, "Figured I could rap (write) better than these crackers can talk over the phone."

Concluded this five-week session tonite on very positive note. During the last five weeks been working with cinquain and Japanese haiku. Hersey Boyer and Jamal wrote play and short stories, respectively. Boyer's first playwrighting attempt shows promise. Suggested he rewrite for possible production by Black Drama Workshop in Buffalo. Jamal's grammar and construction too poor to aid his craft in the short story. I shall return 10/2/73. Really had a fine discussion about poetic values and criticism. Also listened to and criticized Nikki Giovanni's recording *Like a Ripple on a Pond*. This group seems a little more mature in outlook and treated Nikki and Booker T. Washington rather objectively. That is, they felt that both figures did what was best for them at a point in history.

On bus sponsored by BUILD organization heading for Attica for memorial services. I am one of the speakers. A bit concerned about what I shall say and what poems of the Attica workshop I shall read—planning now.

. . . Back on bus after rally which was orderly and one of the most moving experiences of my life. Especially moving was Mrs. Barkley's speech regarding her son's (L. D. Barkley) death during the Attica situation of 9/9–13/71, and the conditions of our society and Attica.

Noticed many T.V. cameras and pictures taken from the walls of Attica—interesting!

September 11, 1973

Attica memorial Rally at Erie Community College (City) at which I read Attica poems. Met Deloris Costello, Station WBAI in N.Y.C., who wants to do a program featuring the book.

September 13, 1973

Attica rally at St. John's Baptist Church—mostly white students there—I read poems—'nuff said.

December 12, 1973

Hersey Boyer has been transferred to Greenhaven Correctional Facility outside of Poughkeepsie, New York. He tells me he appreciates my efforts with the workshop and hopes we can keep in touch.

January 2, 1974

Returned tonite after one-month layoff to find group quite small, only six men of whom only two have done new work. Many other members have been transferred to other prisons or released. Others are involved in college programs within the facility during the same time as the workshop, 6:30–9:00 p.m.

There is not so much lack of interest as there is a lack of ability among the current members. However, Alexander Brooks is a standout in that he is quite familiar with the mechanics of poetry and is the most articulate of all the men I have ever had. Frankly, I thought his ability and facility with words and speech was put on at first, but now I see that his work is genuine and reflects a knowledge of poetry. There is a fineness about his work unlike any student I have had.

The men have been asking me to bring pictures of my family for the past year. Tonite, I brought some, and they were quite delighted. What an affinity they have for family life! I was surprised at their reaction to my

CELES TISDALE

children in the photos. It was quite unlike what I am accustomed to seeing as men's reactions to children.

January 21, 1974

Just retuned last nite from Detroit where I was making final plans for my book on Attica with the publisher, Dudley Randall, of Broadside Press. The collection of poems by the men in my workshop at Attica will go to the printer in April. Mr. Randall and I spent the weekend deciding on the poems for the anthology—a job. My greatest difficulty was in deciding who not to use because of my closeness to the men.

Mr. Randall is a sensitive and learned man in poetry. We talked quite a bit about publishing, and I had an opportunity to see his office and to run a few delivery errands with him; met his wife, Vivian, for the first time—I did not know whether he was married or not. Funny, I never asked him.

Bought about $16.00 worth of books from Broadside and Vaughn's Book Store where we made a delivery. Especially happy to find Paul Laurence Dunbar's *Strength of Gideon and Other Stories* at Vaughn's.

By the way, it appears that the book title will be changed from *Betcha Ain't* to *Attica: Poems from Within*. Mr. Randall felt that the word "Attica" would be a better selling point—more attractive to the eye in a book store. I disagreed, because my title was more catchy. We'll probably use Mr. Randall's idea—I think he has a good point.

January 22, 1974

Heard from Packwood today, who left John Lee Norris's (former Attica inmate and workshop member) address. He is out. Packwood goes before parole board next week. It was Norris's poem "Betcha Ain't" that inspired title for the book.

Speaking of book, received offer today to publish collection of letters and this diary with a major firm, spoke with agent who is associated with a number of publishers in New York City, and others. I shall send copies (Xeroxed) of letter and diary to her, Friday. She is Larry Robinson's mother. Larry is my office mate.

February 6, 1974

Bad snowstorm today. Could not go to Attica—rescheduled for next Wed. Completed manuscript with intro, acknowledgment, dedication, and autobiography. Feel relieved and proud.

February 13, 1974

Sent all material to Dudley Randall relative to *Betcha Ain't* manuscript. Received call from Jan Robinson, agent handling the Attica diary and letters I have kept. She thinks that there may be a market for a book encompassing the letters and my diary. She is going ahead with the contacting of various publishers. Good possibilities.

Cannot go to Attica today because I am too tired from this week's speaking engagements relative to Black History week.

March 16, 1974

Leonard Mackey tells me that he's come out of Attica knowing some fantastic people—"many of whom may never see the streets again." Attica, he says, changes everyone, their commitments, their future.

April 27, 1974

Heard from Dudley Randall at Broadside Press. Book: *Betcha Ain't: Poems from Attica* ready for release May 15th. I am very, very happy.

May 20, 1974

Received first copy of *Betcha Ain't* from Detroit. Truly ecstatic, proud of my accomplishment. Dudley Randall did a fine job of blending the narrative of my diary with the poetry of the men.

CELES TISDALE

Arrangements have been made for me to speak in the now-famous Shrine of the Black Madonna, pastored by Rev. Cleage, in Detroit on Sunday, June 2, 1974, at 1:00 p.m. I shall read from *Betcha Ain't*. What an honor!

May 21, 1974

Picked up other copies of *Betcha Ain't* at Greyhound Bus Terminal. Now, I really believe that I am in the ranks (smile).

May 29, 1974

Packwood tells me that our Wednesday-night poetry workshops "might have kept a few of us from taking the gun" to relieve stress, frustration. The workshops gave him the confidence to say, "I *am* a poet, and a damn good one!" When I first met Packwood, he was solely an improviser; the workshop has made him more introspective, more philosophical.

June 2, 1974
(Detroit, Michigan: Shrine of Black Madonna Church)

Christianity is palatable! In terms of Black nationalism, Rev. Cleage, in his sermon presently going on, there is a kind of relationship. In fact, the Church is related to what they call Black Christian Nationalism (BCN). Interesting in terms of new Black Arts Movement (painting of Black Madonna during '60s). Cleage is a man I must interview after reading his *Black Messiah*.

June 3, 1974
(Detroit, Michigan)

Radio station WDET waiting for interview about *Betcha Ain't*. Yesterday, spoke before congregation about the book and read the title poem. Sold some copies in basement after service.

Today, read from *Betcha Ain't* at Vaughn's Book Store and sold some autographed copies. Good vibes.

June 9, 1974

Betcha Ain't reception held last nite at Buffalo Urban League—very successful—about 200 people including County Executive Edward V. Regan and Assemblyman Arthur Eve.

June 12, 1974

Returned to Attica for first time since *Betcha Ain't* published. The men were so proud and grateful and really vocalized their approval. Some others came over to the workshop from their regular college class to see the book. I gave everyone a copy of the book. Also gave the two guards a copy (Blacks) and the lieutenant in charge. Strange, I have not heard from Dickinson who is education director and who was sent a copy of the book from Detroit.

We have triumphed, but this is only the beginning of many publications. Sure do wish we could subsidize the program and run it weekly as before. I am waiting for a benefactor.

June 13, 1974

Donald Charles Johnson entered the group after many of the original members had left the workshop. He tells me he feels cheated in missing out on the vibes of the original workshop. Johnson says that for him, his interest in poetry really began when he heard all of us read at the Black Solidarity Day event at the prison. "On that day," he says, "I discovered a brand new form of Soul."

June 18, 1974

Received letters from Leonard Mackey and L. Alexander Brooks praising *Betcha Ain't*. Brooks's letter was especially moving and actually brought a tear to my eye. Brooks is a most lucid writer. Letter dated 6/13/74.

June 21, 1974

Held workshop session which I taped. Men talked about *Betcha Ain't* and read their favorite poems. A really good session.

Heard John "Spider" Martin, former Attica inmate, in concert at University of Buffalo. Austin Cromer sang with the sextet. "Spider" is quite good. I taped about one hour of the concert—good jam! Had not heard "Spider" since Black Solidarity Day at Attica, 11/6/72.

July 17, 1974

Generally, a talk session because only two men present. Communications problem again. Donald White AKA Charles Johnson suggested that when we get together again we need more direct teaching of mechanics of poetry. Yes, the men do want the discipline of a class—will heed his suggestion.

K. E. Moody went with me but had to sit out in car. We went to Rochester to continue plans for August 24th Attica Memorial program in Rochester. Met with Roy Rugless, director of Action for a Better Community (ABC), Reggie McGill, and Ronnie—almost finalized the program and publicity. Will be a dynamite program.

August 7, 1974

Called Attica today to confirm my coming and found that they (the men) were not informed. I stayed home. Maybe, the workshop has run its course. I won't push too much anymore, because I think I have something to offer as a teacher—I do not need to have this feeling of being prostituted.

I shall make one last effort to organize a solid workshop by writing a letter to the education director and to certain men in the workshop such as Charles Johnson (Donald White) and Alex Brooks.

September 15, 1974

Haven't had much to say during past month although much activity. Am working on two more books of poems: *Every Wednesday: More Thoughts from Attica* and an anthology of poems by five local women. I have not decided on a title, yet.

On Friday, 9/13, participated in memorial for Attica in Rochester, New York, at the Zerox Auditorium—dynamite! Cast party was good, too (smile).

September 19, 1974

Received letter from Attica workshop member Alexander Brooks. He is trying to get into graduate school in English at Buffalo State College, and he asked that I speak to Chairman Henry Sustakoski.

I really intend to help Bro. Brooks as I helped Harold Packwood get into college. Brooks is much older and, seemingly, more academically inclined. He should do well. Will see Henry tomorrow.

When the Smoke Cleared

More Poems from Attica

Hersey Boyer

Rain Song

My thoughts fall on the yesterdays
of you.
It's raining
as I remember
you used to like the rain.
On soft summer nights such as this,
you would wear your bright red rain coat
and I my dark brown tweed.
Like children,
we would run and play.
In celebration, we offered up a song.
It's raining.
Who walks with you, tonight?

L. Alexander Brooks

The Hermit's Ghost

His old sheepdog whimpered wild
A half-dozen steps inside
The gate, near the well;
The firewood stood neatly piled
Outside the door
Of the shack where the hermit died

Yesterday at sun-up.
This morning, passing by,
The school bus slowed:
I thought I saw him die
Again. Someone had mowed
The lawn. I wonder why

Its only window stood
Ajar, as though to let the light
Come in, when no one stayed
There anymore. This afternoon
We saw it had been closed tight;
We peeked inside and saw the bed was made.

The Odyssey of Louie Fats

(1 October 1973)

Louie was older
Than I, and he was bigger,
Too; so when he spoke
To me, I listened closely.

We all listened real, real close
When Louie Fats spoke.

It wasn't as though
We were afraid. Oh, yes; we were—
But that wasn't it:
Louie Fats was our leader;
He'd been all over the world;
He'd seen everything,

And we'd seen nothing.
(We hadn't even seen things
That happened right there
In Brooklyn, let alone Queens,
Manhattan, or in The Bronx,
The way Louie had.)

Louie had traveled
All over New York City—
I mean *all over*!
He knew streets you couldn't find
On no map, or in no book,
Where the Sun got lost

Just going down them,
And it would be days or weeks
Coming out again;
They have streets like that, you know.
(At least they did in my time;
You mean they don't still?)

When Louie came back
From seeing the world, we knew
He would soon tell us
All the very latest things
He'd seen, and places he'd been.

We could hardly wait . . .

     *

Wall Street, Wall Street, ain't got a wall,
But it got new buildings fifty stories tall,
And people losing money when the market fall,
And jumpin' out windows; but that ain't all

They do, 'cause the market mostly rise.
(You can tell 'cause the men get a gleam in their eyes,
The girls sound excited gulping milk and pies,
And the cops don't chase you, which is quite a surprise.)

That's where Louie Fats used to go,
And how he got to know Delmonico
From the door on Hanover Square, at least, though
He had to admit he really didn't know
What people did there; and he still don't know.

     But he knew that the people who came and went
     Were all upon mighty errands bent,
     For they dressed and acted kind of different
     And talked in a hard-to-understand accent
     About how much the missus had gone out and spent,
     And how high the landlord had raised the rent
     That it was hard to afford a Palm Beach apartment
     Anymore. Louie knew what all that meant:
     Rich people could talk all day and invent;
     There wasn't that much money in the whole U.S. Mint!

     *

Louie got confused when he came to the club.
The sign said it was
THE WEST SIDE TENNIS CLUB,
But it wasn't on the West Side,

Nor even on the East Side;
It was on the Outside,
Way out in Queens, and to get Inside,
You had to have
                a clean white shirt,
You had to have
                bright white teeth,
You had to be
                seven times white
With an English-born white chauffeur
To drive your shiny big black Cadillac; and,

It was in Forest Hills,
With very few trees
And not the first hill,
And people going in and out
Were all old and fat,
Or old and old,
And much, much too old
To play tennis; and besides,
They weren't dressed for it.

Oh, yes: The cop chased him.   Twice.

            *

If you stood at a certain spot on Bedford Avenue
Which, before they tore it down,
Was where the three hundred ninety-nine foot sign
Hung out in right-center field—
        There's a telephone booth there now;
        The phone never works, and the booth
        Smells like . . . I couldn't tell you; I don't know that smell
—Out there you could see Pete Reiser, Dixie, and Medwick,
With only a concrete wall between you and them
And all the cheering, the excitement, the thrill
Of Whitlow Wyatt's fastball fanning Mize,

Camilli, snatching a wide throw, and Riggs at bat,
And Casey coming in to get the side out—
     That was a boy's stolen moment
     Of terrible pleasure, greater
     Than an entire bushel
     Of Forbidden Fruit!
                  Please, Dixie, please!
Please, just this time, when Morton Cooper throws
That ball up to the plate, please, Dixie, please,
If you don't ever get another hit again,
Please, belt it out here onto Bedford Avenue
And let it land right at my feet! Please, Dixie!

     *

It surprised Louie
There were so many people
Flying in airplanes.
He'd heard of Roscoe Turner,
Rickenbacker and Wiley Post,

And Lindbergh, of course,
And he knew they flew in planes;
But he'd never known
Of anybody who flew
As a passenger, except

Roosevelt, Churchill,
And other important men,
Like Joe Louis and . . .
Maybe Bob Feller—maybe.
Where were all of them going?

(Today an airplane
Is just lots of noise; but when
He was still a boy,

A plane was an adventure
Beyond all imagining,

And to see, not one,
But dozens of planes landing,
Taking off, landing,
Hour after hour after hour,
Was enough for ten lifetimes.)

Colonial up!
Capitol waiting to land!
Transcontinental
Waiting for clearance—over!
It's like Coney Island on

The Fourth of July,
Magic Land of LaGwadda,
All come together:
Big as an apartment house—
Gee, I wish I could fly one!

(You'll never get me in one!)

          *

Miss H-6703 was her name.
Maybe it wasn't her name,
At least not her real name;
But it was the only name he knew
Because that was all there was
Printed on the button that she wore:
"H-6703 U.S. NAVAL SHIPYARD
BROOKLYN, N.Y."
It might not have been her name,
But it was *her*, and she knew it.
(Once he'd called it out loud

And she'd turned her head.)
He was sure she was the prettiest woman
In the whole world, after his mother,
His older sister, Rosetta, and his brother Alfred's girl,
Susanna; yes, she was almost as pretty
As Susanna when she—Susanna—frowned.
But she was still very pretty,
Miss Sweet H-6703.

She worked from Eight to Four
When she wasn't working some other shift;
She built big aircraft carriers to sail
Right clear into Tokyo Bay
With Flying Fortresses on her flight deck
That would bomb Tojo, Hirohito, and all the Japs
So bad that they'd wish they'd never heard
Of Pearl Harbor or Bataan, or that they'd gotten
General MacArthur so mad when they chased him out
That he'd sworn on the radio, "I shall return."
She was a beauty. She was a she-ro.
She was so sweet, and good, and pretty,
All her big brothers worried about her
And came to meet her at the gate
By Vanderbilt Avenue and Flushing;
And when one couldn't come, why, another would:
They loved their pretty little she-ro sister.

She came from a big family, and had lots of brothers.

      *

It cost a nickel to get on the train
If you were one to pay the fare, but he,
Who seldom had a nickel he could spare
(And never would have paid it if he had
Had it to spare) knew perfectly well how
To ride for free. It cost a little pride,

If you were one to mind that sort of thing,
But he wasn't; if anything his pride
Expanded in the knowledge of how much
He'd beaten them just picking off the ground
A paper transfer from the Franklin El
Or from the Independent Subway Line —
It didn't matter which, though he preferred
To start out on the El; he liked to look,
And there was more to look at in the light,
Although he could see some things in the dark
That others never saw, and just as plain
As in the light. He liked to stand up front
Where the train engineer rode; he could see
All the strangeness rushing headlong at him,
So that he felt like he was on the tip
Of a great arrowhead, speeding New-ward,
Faster than he had ever felt himself
Moving before. Next after flying planes,
The best thing was to ride the front of trains:
Church, Newkirk, Kings Highway, and Sheepshead Bay —
He thought he might go fishing here one day
Soon, If he didn't venture somewhere else;
And Erie Basin was a name he thought
He liked the sound of, but he didn't know
Just what it was, and no one else he knew
Had even heard of it, unless . . . Unless
He'd gone clear out the country to a lake
That had that name; but it was all the way
By Pearl Harbor, and probably had Japs
Up in the thousands all around, though he
Was very sure he'd seen no Japs around,
And that he'd somehow gotten out unseen
By them, except that he had never been
To that-there Erie-place, he'd only passed
Nearby, deep underground and Japs can't see
Too well in darkness. And someday he meant
To get off at Columbia and ask

If he could talk to Professor Einstein,
Or Thomas Edison, Louis Pasteur,
Or anybody free at the moment
If Dr. Einstein happened to be at
The West Side Tennis Club in Forest Hills.
But most of all he liked crossing the Bridge;
He could look down and see the very ship
Miss H-6703 helped to build,
Or one of the Queens coming up the Bay,
Or the Statue of Liberty, way, way
Away off in the distance. He was thrilled
By the view of ten thousand lantern lights
Publishing to the world the fated news:
The Yanks are coming and they won't be back . . .
They won't be back, they won't be back, . . . They won't . . .
They won't . . . They won't . . . They won't be back until . . .
. . . Until . . . They won't . . . until . . . they won't . . . until . . .
He didn't want to cry and ruin his trip
(He couldn't cry because he was a man.)
But the Bridge saddened him in a strange way
He couldn't explain, since he loved the Bridge
Above all other things he'd ever seen;
He always would, and it would always be
The thunderstone to curb the wild in him
And draw him home again. (Even today,
Although it takes him much out of his way,
He rides the Sea Beach to Pacific Street
And takes the West End Express back again;
It's only fifteen minutes from Canal,
Which isn't far to go to see a friend
You've known since childhood, when you bear in mind
He cannot make the trip so well as you,
Or tell someone, "Give my regards to Lou!")

     *

It all came back together again, there
Where the boats landed. In an hour's time
The whole world came to work in New York Town,
The whole world came home to America,
Saying grace in a thousand tongues unknown,
Or sending him away with eyes that said,
"You there, you don't belong here, can't you see?
Look, and you'll see a thousand-score of me
For every one of you." But most of them
Looked over him, and past him, and through him
Without response, as though they didn't see
Him; that he understood and didn't mind:
Sometimes he looked and never found himself,
And he knew where to look; no wonder then
That he could stand unseen amid the crowd.
One day he took the ferry to St. George.
(He did not pay; a nickel was too much
To give away for nothing if you knew
How you could ride for nothing.) He stood there,
Looking around. It seemed a lonely place,
With nothing there; it looked like parts of Queens
(The way he thought that Brooklyn must have looked
When there were Indians still living there.)
If he went far enough from where he stood
He might see cowboys rounding up their herds,
And Cavalry protecting the settlers.
Next time he came here he would remember
To wear a gun like everybody else
Probably did; but in his heart he thought
He would not come to Staten Island much,
Unless Buck Jones rode as his trail partner.

              *

I think that when a boy becomes a man,
The world becomes a smaller place for him,

The cup is always filled up to the brim,
And he has always done the most he can;
The streets are rutted, and the subway cars
Are dirty and crowded beyond bearing,
The din of protest too loud for hearing.
(They sent a Mariner to orbit Mars.)

But Louie Fats had traveled farther than
The ten thousand generations of Man
Have traveled since Creation first began;
And he did that before he was a man,
Yet, being now a man, can do no more
(Indeed, far less!) that would have satisfied
Him then; and all the things he would have tried
Once, wiser now, he hesitates before.
The brave men of this life have all died young,
Before sixteen; and the last challenge flung
When, in those famous words of long ago,
The fear of fear was all the fear to know.

I think Odysseus, too, was a boy
On his adventures, or he would have been
Afraid to play Queen Circe's human toy,
The danger of it would have pricked him keen.
Sometimes I think of riding at the head
Of trains, if only people wouldn't stare
As though I were new-risen from the dead,
A fourteen-year-old crowned with whitened hair;
I'd like to show them Louie Fats alive
In me; but I have seen so much I know
There are so many places yet to go,
Too many worlds beyond the will to strive.

Chico (Ronald Williams)

ATTICKA ATTICKA

    Breeding ground, fertile prey for unrealized dreams
    that blossom like sun rays on brittle concrete
    igniting passions whose only release are shadows
    casting giant reflections on hollow hopes
        and yesterdays that never came.
ATTICKA: oasis before the body shrivels and mind lapses into
    nothingness of wanted, but never had; before the final
    touch of never feeling.
ATTICKA: to whose futility we succumb and struggle vainly to
    reach the summit of another desire.
ATTICKA: final hatebox for love hats never worn, but used as tools
    in a trade we never mastered; whose brim drips sweatsmiles
    at us being the best but the worst on the shelf.
Our only defense: the fear of a second skin
        whose flesh — scarred carcass
            we erect daily into a higher mountain
        that was built through the me's
            whose graffiti defaces the south wall of you's.
ATTICKA: stone-cold granite
        mirrors humanity's images
    of which we've never been a part
    and whose inhumanity is canvas
        for life's cruel art:
            ATTICKA.

Joseph Hardy

Synopsis of a Hummingbird

In a garden I sat
amid myriad nature faces
A fledging engrossed in thought, when
I first saw the

                                  Humming Bird.

Each morning I came, sat beneath
the tree to capture this mystery.
A move, reach, and it was gone.
And, one day, beneath the tree,
He lay colorless.

Jamal Ali Bey Hassan

Rise On

Rise on beautiful queen of a smoldering city,
Rise on to the height of a new people.
Your people, my people, black people.

Oh lovely woman, lead the people,
For we are your children,
Rise on Mother Africa, rise on.

Rise on daughters of the earth,
Give birth to the man child,
And with your love teach them,
Teach them that this land is ours.

I am one of your own in a far-off land
Searching for myself.
But you have come to me on the wing,
And so I say, Rise on my mother, Rise on.

Leonard C. Mackey

Mercy Killing

The world
totters from the twentieth-century malignancy
and Nature is bent.

The bomb
now seems a blessing
to save us from our
last
mad
moments.

City Interlude

In the midst of
     noise
         and
             hurry
               and
                   grimy streets
sits the Art Museum
     serene, spacious—
Oasis
     in a paved desert.

John Lee Norris

/PRISON POETS/

black
poems
about
prisons
should have   teeth that bite,
and
black
poets
in
prisons   should bite ass
and
pile
zebra
stripes
bodiesbetweenthelines

A Stretch-Sketch

And I said I am a man!
                              /and the judge said 50 years.
Having
been
Eaten up by time
Sitting here in this tomb
                    Watching brainless flies
                              ZIG ZAG
        Across steel bars and concrete floors.
I am weary   but strong
              So strong

That my thoughts sprout wings
        Carrying my Black spirit
    Over these high gray walls
        This man-made hell
        This cruel concrete and steel
                that incarcerates
My being
My manhood
My human right
        to be as free as the black birds that
              fly past this barred
Window!

Harold E. Packwood

Weekend in a Springhill Mine

(For Richard Brautigan)

Saturday-Sunday,
   Lost in a thought mine
Read and laughed,
Wrote and remembered,
Went to sleep and dreamt about
That horse that had a flat tire.

Morning-morning,
My stomach growled.
   /Gas tank empty—I went to breakfast,
Alone—
Watched over by blue machines of loving grace.

The Battle of Joe Meek

Common labor,
Don't pay too good.
And sixteen hours lifting hot steel
Don't leave much time for love,
Or kindness.
Overtime is a way of life,
Leaving eight hours in the day
To satisfy that fine brown chick
Now growing weary
From a particular loneliness
And the day screaming children
Who multiply
Faster than you get that been-waiting-for raise.

Bringing home the bacon
Always leaves short money,
And what do you tell
Seven child-black faces
Who believe in Santa Claus?

Steelmill machines whisper
In her voice,
        "Joe, Joe, Joe baby!"
But you're too tired,
Muscles aching—can't move
To fulfill her need.
Foremen in white shirts beneath iron hats
Peeking through pale faces,
Gray eyes scorning your greasy Levi's,
Softly demanding—commanding,
Joe, do this—Joe, do that!
Giving you the good-nigger wink,
And your blood boils,
But you take it out on her
With brutal blows and harsh words,
Then weep in her arms;
Body racking sobs saying—"I'm sorry."
Tenderly she strokes your hair
Like a child—until she comes;
But she stares at the ceiling all night.

Hot metal blistering your hands,
Iron stench in your nose;
Pulling another overtime
Till the Charlie whistle frees the slaves.

Moving through an empty house,
No family sounds,
No childish laughter—ain't nobody home;
Short note on a rent receipt
Leaves you momentarily stunned,

Then the horror and the fear
Rise in your throat
As you vomit unheard words of anguish,
"No, mutha-fucka—No!"

Blindly;
You search for something—anything!

Out into the streets you run
Fury on two legs
And the niggers scream,
        "Lookout—Joe Meek's got a gun,"
            "Joe Meek's got a gun!"
                Mutha-fucka,
                    BANG!!!
            "Joe Meek's got a gun!"

Sounds of Silence

Love is gone,
Lost in poverty's shadow.
In the solitude—I cry,
For the days of childhood;
        When we were young,
I dreamed,
In our blackness,
Love would last—poverty would cease,
But the streets are poor,
And I am of the marriage,
Still searching,
        Amid the sounds of silence.

"The Death of Bang-Bang Charlie"

Bang-Bang Charlie—
Was a mean son-of-a-bitch;
Notched his gun on weekends,

Killed—Monday to Friday,
Eight hours a day.
A sky-blue gunfighter
Straight from Dodge City
Or some upstate cornfield,
Riding his Ford Mustang.
Badge gleaming from his hat
Like a mod Wyatt Earp,
Totin' his Colt .45 Hickory Stick
And chewin' Beech-Nut Bubblegum.
Rode into town on Festival Day
Shootin' meanies at the crowd,
His pink mouth lost in a snarl-dripping water,
'Cause he wanted some fried chicken too.
Reached for his gun
When six strangers came to town,
Black faces and power signs,
Lookin' like they been frownin' since birth.
Opened their cases and pulled out their killing machines
Shining in the sunlight,
And the crowd roared
To hear the bullets fly.
The Black sounds echoed and laughed,
Cried—screamed—killing us all
To be born again;
Then Archie Shepp drew his Soprano Sax,
And Bang-Bang Charlie had a heart attack.

Shadows

Wine-stained
stoops
Leading oddly
to the ground
Kissing
cracked concrete
Like ancient lovers,

Toothless
signs
and bad breath.
Tiredly,
they embrace
locked in a
death grip
Dying
From too many
Gypsy Rose
bottles,
Burnt
jar tops,
Saturday-night
blood.
Too many
Sons
in jail.
Daughters
night-walking.
Too many
Fears,
And
Tears.

Palm Sunday

Hosanna,
        the little angels sang
As I looked for my sock.
Christ!—I thought,
No wonder he wore sandals:
His donkey would have died
From old age
If he had to find a sock.
Or,
        Maybe he would

Have bought a pair
At John's Bargain Store
                In Jerusalem.
I think
        The one on the Hill
Is open on Sundays.

"Olé"

the wite bull
warily enters
        the dark arena
head lowered
horns flashing/murder
snorting hot
        breath/to
black applause
Coltrane/Dolphy
        Miles
blasting horns
        signal
the silent
        black
matador/No
diamond sequins
        No
suit of lights
draped in
billows
        of black
        cotton
head like/a
black
        mountain ram
graceful strides
to confrontation

Sun Ra
      strikes
      the cosmic/chord
extensions
      of
days/enslaved
      no more
the final
      death game
in the swirling
      dust/patterns
black/wite
      Imamu
are you here?
So short
      the tune
Nihilismus Dada
blood/spots
brown sand
Black Voices
Ring . . .
      Olé!!

Christopher Sutherland

**Applause to
Archie Shepp & Co.**

We listened
To your
rhythmic hope message
That quickly dissolved
Suffocating despair
With fresh air
For all
Your music
Won our hearts
And our souls' applause.

The End of Summer

The end of summer
Swiftly comes the fall
Putting summer's toys away,
The beaches cold, silent
Where we, like children used to play
The carousel is quiet
The Ferris wheel is still
The "Cyclone" is unmoving
Where once we shared a thrill
Closed are the little places
Where we played the games of chance
Silent is the music

Gone is the bee
That to the flowers hummed

And kissed their smiling faces
As he went along
Leaves blush color
Before they say goodbye
Summer's stage deserted
No colorful remnants left
But from my palace of solitude
I'll picture summer, queen
In the album of my mind.

Twelve Past the Hour of Forty-Three: Attica—Sept. 13, 1971

The clock of memory
Creeps around the hands of time
And once again hearts are struck
By the hour of twelve past forty-three
That ushers in a day shorn
Of its virgin pinkish blush
And golden-dressed beginning.
The day begins with abiding
Brooding sadness of yesterday's
Remembered brutal illusion
Of man's innate goodness.
At the appropriate hour of tears
The sky baptizes the bloody stains of writing
Written on blades of grass
Strangled to death
By a poisonous egg
Laid by a mechanical bird.
The harsh thunder of barred doors closing
Assaults the air echoing a dirge
That makes mockery
Of all the reverent, euphonic eulogies.
What song of sorrow can be sung?
What sermon delivered or proper monument raised

In honor of men whose spirits lie in a cold
Sepulcher hermetically sealed against the
Nourishments of human kindness where men were reborn
Men in the minds of men,
But only after death?

Epilogue
Remember
This

(A note on September 9–13, 1971)

Why must we remind the world that
We are men and should be treated as such
Even as we die in our resistance to ominous overtures
That prelude cacophonous symphonies of hatred and death
Or, will there be a coda of hope, an interlude
Before we die again, again.
But, the poet said, "If we must die . . ." —
What will we remember to tell the others who heard
And could not understand why this, why that.
We will say, remember this, and never forget
       The You of You, like men . . .

—Celes Tisdale

Acknowledgments

My sincere thanks to Amber J. Meador and Hadeen Stokes for their assistance in typing and shaping the manuscript. Poet Mark Nowak's insightful comments and editing were most helpful, and Anthony Bannon's artistic acumen influenced me greatly in developing my association with Attica Correctional Facility. Special thanks to the late Dudley Randall, owner of Broadside Press in Detroit, Michigan. Thanks also to the late poet Gwendolyn Brooks, who first "saw something" in what the men in the Attica writers workshop had to say in their poems. I am glad I listened to her and brought the men's poems and my journal to the world. Thank you, Ed Smith, for recommending me to Attica State Prison, and thanks to my son, Angus Wilton McLean III, for his technical assistance.

Appendix
Workshop
Documents

Prof. C. Tisdale

Poetry Workshops

I. Session I—Poetry's Sound (Performance)
   A. Listen for Poetic Elements:
      1. Rhyme (sometimes)
      2. Rhythm
      3. Mood
      4. Imagery ("Word Pictures")
      5. Setting
   B. Poems Recited
      1. "Good Morning Daddy"—Langston Hughes (Rhythm)
      2. "Rivers"—Langston Hughes (Subtle rhythm/mood)
      3. "Ballad of the Landlord"—Langston Hughes (Rhyme)
      4. "Molly Means"—Margaret Walker (Mood/narrative)
      5. "The Creation"—James Weldon Johnson (Imagery)
      6. "The Raven"—Edgar Allan Poe (Imagery)
      7. "Feed My Cow" (Play Song, traditional)
      8. "Casey at the Bat"—Ernest Lawrence Thayer (Setting)
      9. Assign—Sequel to "Casey at the Bat" for Session I
II. Session II—What Is Poetry? (Review of Performance)
   A. Compare with Prose
   B. Elements of Poetry (review)
      1. Rhyme (sometimes)
      2. Rhythm
      3. Mood
      4. Imagery ("Word Pictures")
      5. Setting (Place, time)

C. Students Read Sequels to "Casey at the Bat" & Discussion

D. Prof. Tisdale Reads "Casey's Revenge" by James Wilson & Discussion

E. Assign—Give copies of "Casey at the Bat" & "Casey's Revenge" to each student

    1. Students underline unknown/unfamiliar words

    2. Students establish setting—why?

    3. Could story be true? Why? Why not?

    4. Elements of folklore? (Hero story)

III. Session III—"Mechanics of Poetry"

A. Discussion Session II Assignment

B. Review copies of "Molly Means" by Margaret Walker and "The Raven" by Edgar Allan Poe

    1. Imagery

    2. Assonance

    3. Metaphor

    4. Mood

C. Introduce Haiku

D. Assign—Write a haiku

IV. Poetry Types

A. Haiku

    1. Review haiku (students read originals) discussion

    2. Write group haiku

B. Cinquain

    1. Show similarity to haiku

    2. Write group cinquain

C. Limerick

    1. Note humor "gone wild" with examples

    2. Discuss elements and variations

D. Assign:

    1. Write original cinquains

    2. Write original limericks

V. Session V—Techniques of Poetry Reading (Oral)

A. Choice of material (understanding)

    1. Audience

    2. Purpose

B. Use of Body

    1. Voice pitch/dynamics

    2. Diction/pronunciation

    3. Eye contact

    4. Gestures

C. Review/discuss original cinquains and limericks

VI. Session VI—Summary
    A. Shakespearean Sonnet
    B. General Review
    C. "The Creation"—James Weldon Johnson
        1. To show all elements of poetry discussed
        2. To introduce mythology/folklore

Attica State Correctional Facility
Black Poetry Workshop, Phase II

TEXT: *THE BLACK POETS* —
Dudley Randall, Editor (Bantam Press, New York, 1971)

August 9, 1972 — I.   Discussion of Goals and Requirements
II. Introduction of Each Workshop Member
III. What Is Poetry? (discussion)
IV. Assign Poem to be Written for Next Session and Give Text

August 16, 1972 — I.   History of Black Poetry from Ancient Africa to Present (lecture, readings, discussion)
II. Each Member Reads Original Poem (discussion)
III. Assign Poems from Text for Discussion Next Session

August 23, 1972 — I.   Discussion of Assigned Poems from Text
II. Recorded Poetry—"Truth Is On Its Way" Nikki Giovanni (Right-on Records RR05001)
III. Assign Text "Introduction" thru page 56 for Next Session

August 30, 1972 — I.   Poetic Devices:
Imagery, Metaphor, Simile, Symbol, Alliteration, Assonance, Personification, Onomatopoeia, Anthropomorphism, Hyperbole (refer to examples in text)
II. Discussion of Assignment (see last week) and Introduce Harlem Renaissance
III. Assign pgs. 57–101: "Harlem Renaissance"

NO SESSION SEPTEMBER 6, 1972

September 13, 1972 — I.   Poetic Types:
Ballad, Narrative, Sonnet, Ode, Japanese Haiku, Cinquain, Limerick (refer to examples reprinted for each member)
II. The Harlem Renaissance (lecture, readings, discussion)
III. Discuss Assignment (see last week)

September 20, 1972 — I. The Harlem Renaissance (conclusion)
II. Discuss Assignment (see last week)
III. Don L. Lee (taped recording-discussion)
IV. Assign: Pgs. 181–187; 203–227; 231–242; 284–289; 295–309; 318–329; "The Nineteen Sixties"

September 27, 1972 — I. Joint Meeting of Both Attica Workshop Groups 6–9 p.m.
Imamu Amiri Baraka (LeRoi Jones)
Taped Recording: "Nguzo Saba"
II. Buffalo Black Writers Workshop "Rap" Session and Poetry Reading with Members of Attica and Buffalo Workshops

October 4, 1972 — I. Joint Meeting of Both Attica Workshop Groups 6–9 p.m.
Recorded Poetry—"The Last Poets" (Pip Records—Douglas Recording Corp.)—Discussion
II. Evaluation of Eight-Week Session with Workshop Members

NOTE: All members will be required to present some form of original work done during the preceding week at each session.

Celes Tisdale
Workshop Director

Sponsored by Buffalo Black Drama Workshop through a grant from New York State Council on the Arts, and in cooperation with Hospital Audiences, Incorporated.

TIS-O-GRAM

(An Exercise Comparing Abstract Ideas/Emotions with Concrete Examples)

	Concrete Example					
Abstract Idea	Looks Like	Smells Like	Tastes Like	Sounds Like	Feels Like (to touch)	Color
LOVE						
HATE						
COURAGE						
FEAR						
JOY						
DISAPPOINTMENT						
ACCEPTANCE						
REJECTION						
PAIN						
RELIEF						
ANXIETY						
FAITH						
EXPECTATION						
ENERGY						
EXHAUSTION						
TRUST						
SUSPICION						
LAUGHTER						
SADNESS						
WEALTH						
POVERTY						
PEACE						
WAR						
CALM						
VIOLENCE						

Note: Responses should be one word; no response should be used more than once.